THE ECONOMIC CONSEQUENCES
OF THE
VIETNAM WAR

The Economic Consequences of the Vietnam War

Anthony S. Campagna

PRAEGER

New York
Westport, Connecticut
London

Library of Congress Cataloging-in-Publication Data

Campagna, Anthony S.
    The economic consequences of the Vietnam war / Anthony S.
Campagna.
        p. cm.
    Includes bibliographical references and index.
    ISBN 0–275–93816–6 (alk. paper). — ISBN 0–275–93388–1 (pbk. :
alk. paper)
    1. Vietnamese Conflict, 1961–1975—Economic aspects—United
States.   2. United States—Economic conditions—1961–1971.
3. United States—Economic conditions—1971–1981.   I. Title.
HC106.6.C287   1991
973.923—dc20   90–45296

British Library Cataloguing in Publication Data is available.

Library of Congress Catalog Card Number: 90–45296
ISBN: 0–275–93816–6
        0–275–93388–1 (pbk.)

First published in 1991

Praeger Publishers, One Madison Avenue, New York, NY 10010
An imprint of Greenwood Publishing Group, Inc.

Printed in the United States of America

∞

The paper used in this book complies with the
Permanent Paper Standard issued by the National
Information Standards Organization (Z39.48–1984).

10 9 8 7 6 5 4 3 2 1

For my father,
who knew some of the words,
and for my mother, who did not.

CONTENTS

TABLES

PREFACE

Analysis of the Vietnam War has really just begun—some 15 years after the war's ignoble end. Only now can we begin to attempt to measure the impact of that tragic undertaking on the social, political, and economic structures of the United States. That American society was disrupted in every way seems scarcely debatable. The war, however, generated too much heat for dispassionate analysis while it was being fought and was far too controversial for calm reasoning to emerge for some time after it was finished. Perhaps hindsight will afford us the perspective necessary for less emotional investigations.

Much, of course, has already been written about both the societal disruptions caused by the exodus of young men to Canada and the plight of the returning vet to a society that could not honor his efforts. Families were disrupted. Honest men learned how to lie to avoid combat. Colleges were bulging with escapees while minorities learned once again that they were expendable. Political careers were made or broken. Military men found the avenue to advance their careers.

The effects upon us will be told again and again by creative people who will write the novels and plays, produce the TV programs, or paint the pictures to show us the pieces of horror that comprise a war. But they will fail, as others before them have failed, to convince us of the futility of it all. Each generation conveniently forgets the lessons and provides seemingly fresh rationales for setting caution and reason aside as it invents new excuses, exaggerates threats, and supplies bogus explanations to cover ulterior motives.

The war in Vietnam was no different. It had its own justification, its own rationale, and its own internal logic to play out once it began. However, it is not the purpose of this book to elaborate on these issues nor to discuss the myriad social consequences that ensued once it ended. Others are better equipped to handle that task. Nevertheless it will be impossible to avoid some discussion, however summarily, of these issues in the course of pursuing our main purpose.

The purpose of this book is comparatively modest: to examine the economic impact of the Vietnam War on the U.S. economy. This might appear to be a straightforward task, but that is not the case. In the first place, the economic impact ought to include benefits as well as costs. But benefits are always more difficult to account for than costs, a problem common to cost-benefit analysis. In the second place, some costs are recorded and readily identified, while others are indirect or extend far into the future. Even if one is successful in distinguishing costs and accounting for benefits, a full accounting of them may never be possible for there are too many that are immeasurable.

These difficulties require that the economic impact of the war be concentrated more on the cost side and that the economic consequences of the war be viewed from two perspectives: the short run and the long run. In the short run, the costs of the war are considered in the light of how they affected the performance of the U.S. economy. Additional spending on defense can be expected to cause repercussions in the domestic economy. Inflation is the partner of war, and economic policies must be designed to deal with the problem. Other stresses and strains on an economic system are also caused by wars, and these too require policy actions.

So the first task is to explain how the economy was affected by the Vietnam War over time and to outline the short run economic policies followed in response. This procedure allows for the interesting comparison of the development of the war with that of the economy that was affected by it. It is interesting also to witness the political dilemmas posed for policymakers with an unpopular war amid domestic dissent and division.

Recording the history of policy-making would be valuable but not sufficient. In response to the effects of the war on the economy, and to public policy reactions, many adjustments were made by the economic agents affected by them. As they sought to free or protect themselves from the economic problems created, people began to change some of the basic institutions in the economy. In fact many initial changes can be observed at the outset of the Vietnam War buildup, around the year 1966. The very structure of the U.S. economy began to change, and this is discussed in the context of transforming the economy and influencing the effectiveness and efficiency of macroeconomic policies thereafter.

Finally the institutional transformation of the U.S. economy has longer-run consequences that must be determined. Along the way some of the short-term changes were discarded or were temporary. These changes must be separated from those that can be expected to affect the operation of the economy for years after the original change occurred. Thus some of the long-run consequences of the war-induced adjustments are suggested.

In summary, the main thrust of this study is to identify some of the immediate economic consequences of the war and to show how those consequences led to adjustments in the economic system that were severe enough to warrant the claim that the economic structure was transformed. The postwar economy would never be the same as the prewar economy, and furthermore, there would be no tendency to return to the earlier economic structure. There are no internal mechanisms to steer the economy back to its original path of development.

Given the main focus of the book, it seems logical to structure it in such a way that it addresses costs and benefits in a sequential manner. Thus Part I is concerned with the early involvement in the war up through the Kennedy administration. The description of the state of the economy prior to the war, in the early stages of the conflict, is a necessary preliminary before addressing the war's impact as it progressed. Part II focuses on the military buildup as it occurred in the Johnson and Nixon administrations. The war's impact on the economy and the policy responses are discussed in terms of how they were conducted by each administration. This economic record of the war years is interrupted and supplemented by the factors that caused changes in the economic structure. The transformed economy begins to affect the policy-making in the latter half of the period, and this is outlined. In Part III, the costs and benefits of the war are included, along with some of the longer-term economic consequences. Finally a look at the post-Vietnam society is undertaken in order to provide some insight into some of the longer-run repercussions on both the society and the economy. The oil embargo, the Vietnam syndrome, and reactions to them are shown as examples of seemingly unconnected threads from the wartime economy.

It is difficult to be unbiased in an analysis of this kind. I was opposed to the war from its very beginning, but that is not the reason for writing this book, nor does that admission affect my analysis in a serious way. Rather I find the reactions of an economy to such a socially disrupting event to be intriguing; to discover in retrospect the changes in the economic structure, the institutional innovations, the behavioral responses, and so on that ensued from the war is the attraction for me. In the book I use the pebble in the water metaphor to describe the kinds of repercussions that are possible when the economy is disturbed by significant events. The economy, like the water, never returns to its original position. The U.S. economy never did return to its former structure because significant changes had been made that prevented it from doing so.

To describe all of these changes, even if we could identify them all, would take a lifetime of study. I merely wished to identify some of the major changes, and to suggest some of the others. There are no proofs here, no technical virtuosity displayed to attempt rigorous exercises to support all of the arguments and assertions made. Whenever the analysis gets too technical or esoteric, the arguments are made in the notes to the chapter. Had this book been written for the professional economist, it would have been a far different one. My aim was to reach a wider audience, and to avoid the jargon of the profession or its badges of sophistication. Indeed most of the discussion is suggestive rather than scholarly and complete. Most of the evidence supplied is not original, and many of the arguments made are not either. Many people have written about various aspects of the economic effects of the war, and their work is heavily utilized and acknowledged. Without their work this book would not have been possible, or if possible, not nearly as comprehensive.

What I wanted to achieve was to bring all the evidence together, and to maintain that when one looks at the total picture, a different view emerges: that the economy was fundamentally changed by the war in Southeast Asia, and the repercussions were many and varied. Indeed many still have not been identified.

I also should like to acknowledge and thank two reviewers, unknown to me, who made valuable suggestions for improvements in the manuscript. I followed many of their suggestions, and the book is a better one for it. I may regret that I did not pursue all of their comments, but in any case they are, of course, not responsible for any errors or omissions in the book.

The war affected everyone in some manner, and I am no exception. Thus on a personal level, I write with the anguish of one who was and still is both angered and disturbed that such a foolhardy conflict could ever have been undertaken: that people of reason could be beguiled into supporting such an adventure and supplying the necessary justifications, even when they had to fool themselves first. If this book does anything to prevent such a recurrence, it will be justified on that score alone.

I   Early Involvement in Southeast Asia

1 THE INITIAL YEARS
The Eisenhower and Kennedy Administrations

U.S. involvement in Vietnam began when the Truman administration promised to help the French continue their control in Indochina. Following World War II, successive U.S. presidents maintained, in one form or another, that the United States was responsible for order in the world. Part of Truman's foreign policy, evident in Southeast Asia, was the containment of communism. In Asia, this meant the Chinese communists, who could presumably control the Vietnamese, notwithstanding the fact that the Chinese and the Vietnamese had been enemies for centuries.

The commitment to colonialism continued in the Eisenhower administrations with the direct support of the French in the form of weapons, equipment, and technical help. Eisenhower considered the need to do more than just aid the French in their struggle but was very reluctant to intervene alone, and when the British rebuffed all attempts to get involved, he abandoned this more direct route. After Korea, Eisenhower was not eager to confront the Chinese again.[1] Still he predicted that were the communists to win in Vietnam, other countries would "topple like a row of dominoes."[2]

Charles E. Wilson, secretary of defense in Eisenhower's first term, stated in his *Semiannual Report* that:

In September 1953, $385 million were allocated to the direct support of the French Union Forces and added to the $400 million previously appropriated for this purpose in the budget for fiscal year 1954. These amounts were in addition to the regular Indochinese military assistance program for weapons and equipment, the delivery of which maintain in operational order the major weapons and equipment supplied by the United States. During the emergency in May 1954,

United States Air Force transports rushed troop reinforcements from France to Indochina.[3]

Additional military assistance was provided under the Military Assistance Program, under the 1954 Agricultural Trade and Development Act (Public Law 480)[4], and under the Mutual Security Appropriations Act for 1955 ($700 million). When Congress became more anxious over the amounts being spent in Vietnam as it was considering the fiscal year 1966 budget, these funds were transferred from assistance programs to other appropriations accounts. At that time, a full accounting of the amounts spent was requested and revealed the data provided in Table 1.1.

Clearly the amounts involved, some $2.4 billion over a dozen fiscal years, would not have been sufficient to affect the economy in a serious way, and the impact could be expected to be minimal. To illustrate, even at the peak of spending in Vietnam in these early years, the amounts represent only 0.04 percent of the GNP and 0.53 percent of national defense spending. (But note how much larger the amounts are when compared to the Reagan administration's "success" at getting Congress to appropriate funds for the Contras in Nicaragua amounting to $100 million out of a defense budget of $273 billion in 1986.)

Table 1.1
Economic Aid for Vietnam (in Millions of Dollars)

Fiscal Year	Agency for International Development and Other Agencies	Public Law 480 (all titles)	Total
1953–57	783.9	39.4	823.3
1958	179.1	9.7	188.8
1959	200.6	6.5	207.1
1960	169.0	11.5	180.5
1961	132.6	12.0	144.6
1962	110.7	32.5	143.2
1963	133.2	64.3	197.5
1964	159.3	71.0	230.3
1965	216.1	52.8	268.9
Total	2,084.5	299.7	2,384.2

Source: Leonard B. Taylor, *Financial Management of the Vietnam Conflict, 1962–1972* (Washington, D.C.: Department of the Army, 1974), 23.

It is apparent, however, that these data do not include the cost of military personnel in Vietnam. In the early Eisenhower years, from 1954–60, an average of 650 troops was assigned to Vietnam but when he was leaving office in 1961, the number had grown to 773; for fiscal year 1961, his last budget year, the number had grown even further to over 1,000.[5] Murray Weidenbaum has estimated that at $23,000 per soldier, the cost to the U.S. was about $15 million per year during the 1954–60 period, rising to $18 million in fiscal year 1961.[6] Weidenbaum does not reveal how he arrived at the cost per soldier of $23,000, but it is close to the estimate given by the Assistant Secretary of Defense Robert N. Anthony. In testimony before the Joint Economic Committee on the effects of Vietnam spending, Anthony gave a "rough" estimate of the cost per soldier of $25,000 to $30,000 per year in Vietnam.[7] Over time the cost of $25,000 became the accepted estimate.

Here, right at the outset, is the appearance of one of the major problems in accounting for the costs of the Vietnam conflict. These personnel costs were not included in the estimates of Table 1.1. As we will see in Chapter 6, many costs were either excluded in the final accounting of war costs, or they were recorded in a misleading and confusing manner. Also the costs were continuously underestimated when they were made public. In fact *official* estimates of the costs of the Vietnam War do not even begin until 1965, although surely there were many expenditures prior to that time. Accounting for the costs of the war will occupy us in Chapter 6, and so it is best to postpone further discussion of costs for the present.

In these early years, the actual amounts, including or excluding personnel costs, were not large enough to alter the conclusion that they probably would not have had a major impact on the U.S. economy. The economy did experience a period of stagnation in the 1950s as three recessions in the Eisenhower years reduced the economic growth rate to 2.4 percent, a full percentage point below the preceding postwar period. There was also much consternation over the fact that the Soviet Union was growing faster economically and technically. When Sputnik I, the Soviet Union's first satellite, was launched in October 1957, there were charges brought of a technology gap. Falling behind in the technological race was a national embarrassment, and soon the educational establishment was blamed for its failures in mathematics and science. The National Defense Education Act was passed quickly to improve teaching in these areas, and later the National Aeronautics and Space Administration (NASA) was formed to close the technology gap in space exploration.

The stable economy of the 1950s was growing slowly, interrupted by three mild recessions, but regardless of the state of the economy, military spending to fend off the encroaching communists in Southeast Asia would not have presented any funding problems, especially in the cold war atmosphere generated by Senator Joseph McCarthy, Sputnik, the Suez Canal crisis, and the whole foreign policy of containment of communism. Interestingly the first recession of 1953–54 was in large part caused by a *reduction* in defense spending on the order of $11 billion, a fact downplayed by the administration. The recession of 1957–58 was due to the turnaround in investment spending on capital goods following the boom in investment in 1955–56. The recovery was not robust, and the economy stagnated into the 1960s with another downturn in 1960–61.

As might be expected, national defense spending rose following the national hysteria over the alleged technological lead of the Soviet Union. From the low of $39 billion in 1955 (9.8 percent of the GNP) national defense purchases rose to $49 billion in 1961 (9.4 percent of the GNP), or in other terms back to where it was before the Eisenhower cuts in 1953. These increases no doubt helped the economy stabilize and might have encouraged growth, but in other areas of fiscal and monetary policy, the Eisenhower administrations were overly conservative, and these increases were offset by reductions in other areas of the budget. Indeed discretionary fiscal policy took a holiday in the Eisenhower years, and only the highway program was initiated. Even here, the program was justified in the name of national defense requirements.

In summary, the assistance given to the French in their colonial war in Indochina did not affect the economy in a significant manner. The amounts were small in relation to the national output and relative to total national defense spending. The willingness to support the French was clearly evident, and most actions, particularly financial, would not have been questioned by the American public, now thoroughly imbued with cold war rhetoric and fearful of communism's expansion and of the Soviet Union's technological advances.

THE KENNEDY ADMINISTRATION

The slowdown in the economy in 1960 helped to elect John F. Kennedy (over Richard Nixon) who capitalized on economic stagnation and "gaps" in economic growth, technology, and missiles. Nixon blamed economic conditions particularly for his defeat as his advice to stimulate the economy prior to the election went unheeded by Eisenhower. One of the means suggested to encourage economic activity was increased spending on national defense.

But it was the Kennedy administration that would follow that advice. Soon after taking office, Kennedy began one of the most rapid military buildups in peacetime and planned increased spending on the Polaris and Minuteman missiles to reduce the alleged missile gap. The gap did not exist but the spending continued anyway, some $17 billion over five years. This exercise in military Keynesianism did not perturb the New Economists who were enticed into public service with their Keynesian views and growth-oriented prescriptions for the economy. However, as is the case for most of national defense budgets, the timing of their effects on the economy is difficult to gauge.

Congressional appropriations for additional defense spending do not indicate any immediate effect on the economy; the funds must first be obligated and spent before they begin to affect the economy. The funds are obligated by the Department of Defense (DOD) when it assigns the funds to areas of expenditure that were authorized by Congress. Here is where the trouble begins; some of these funds are converted to contracts and quickly spent, say on food for the military, but other obligated funds involve equipment or weapons that may take some time to produce and deliver. Only when defense contractors begin to produce the weapon or service and actually pay out wages, rents, interest, and profit is the economy affected. These payments for incomplete goods end up in business inventories, at which time they are properly recognized in the GNP accounts as current production. At this time the economy is affected as wages, interest costs, rents, and profits are paid out and respent, saved, etc.

When the final goods are delivered to the government and finally recorded as *government purchases*, the economic impact has already been felt, and GNP is not affected. (The government purchases are offset by the reduction in inventories.) Yet the state of the economy, and hence economic policy-making, is formed largely by the data in the GNP accounts. In addition to this problem of timing are the problems of progress payments, government provision of facilities, and special arrangements with defense contractors, and the actual timing of the economic impact of defense programs is nearly impossible to determine.[8]

In any event, defense expenditures began to creep upward and government purchases in the national income accounts rose to $52 billion in 1963 or 9.1 percent of the GNP. Kennedy was ambivalent about Vietnam, rejecting large scale U.S. intervention, but reluctant to pull out entirely, supporting the anticommunist movement in Southeast Asia, but rejecting neutrality for South Vietnam. Richard Goodwin writing about this period reminds us that admittedly the line between participation and assistance became thinner, more obscure, as the magnitude of our effort increased. But Kennedy was always careful to draw it. At the end of 1961, Maxwell Taylor, returning from a visit to Vietnam, urged the president to send combat troops—eight thousand at once, and more "if needed," to be accompanied by American bombing of North Vietnam. . . . McNamara enthusiastically supported the Taylor report with the caveat that eight thousand troops would not be enough, but that we could "safely assume the maximum U.S. forces required on the ground will not exceed six divisions or about 250,000 men." (His estimate is an illustration of the wondrously alluring technique of giving a numerical value to a guess derived from speculation informed by ignorance and fueled by desire.) [Parenthesis in the original][9]

Once more heeding the advice of his friend, General Maxwell Taylor, along with advisors such as W. W. Rostow, Kennedy allowed the troop buildup to continue, and by the end of 1963, U.S. military personnel in Vietnam totaled 16,575. At a cost of approximately $25,000 per soldier, this meant an annual cost of $414 million.[10]

Again these costs are not reflected in the *official* Vietnam War costs, and in fact the troop buildup was even hidden from Congress and of course the American public because it violated the Geneva agreement between France and the Democratic Republic of Vietnam (DRVN) limiting the number of new troops permitted in the area. President Kennedy, attempting to forestall an even greater military presence, said with an uncanny prescience, "The troops will march in, the bands will play, the crowds will cheer, and in four days everyone will have forgotten. Then we will be told we have to send in more troops. It's like taking a drink. The effect wears off, and you have to take another."[11]

The defense buildup in the Kennedy years began to affect the national economy. There was, however, still a great deal of slack in the economy that was just emerging from the recession of 1960–61. In the upswing of the previous recession, 1958–60, the Eisenhower administration failed to stimulate the economy by an active discretionary fiscal policy and let the automatic stabilizers work unhindered. In an upswing, the automatic stabilizers act to restrain the economy and create what is called "fiscal drag." When incomes are rising in an upswing, people pay higher taxes on their incomes, unemployment insurance payments fall as people find jobs, welfare payments are reduced, and so on. These effects restrain private spending and take place automatically, without any actions of

Congress. Unless the restraining effects, the fiscal drag, are offset by increased government expenditures or reductions in taxes, the federal budget becomes more and more restrictive over time and can prevent the attainment of full employment.

Thus in 1961, there was a large gap between potential and actual output. One way to measure the extent of the problem is to calculate what the potential output would be at *full employment* with current tax rates and expenditure policies. This procedure eliminates the automatic stabilizers from working (the economy is at full employment). Now it is possible to measure the government's effect on the economy: if the "full employment budget," as it was called at that time, showed a surplus, the government was actually restraining the economy and preventing it from reaching full employment; if the full employment budget showed a deficit, the government was stimulating the economy and pushing it toward full utilization of its resources.

The full employment budget also provided the proper fiscal policy to follow to reach or maintain full employment. For example, the situation facing the Kennedy administration was a full employment surplus of $13 billion (1958 prices) and an unemployment rate of 6.8 percent.[12] Fiscal policy thus called for an increase in expenditures or a reduction of taxes to stimulate the economy, eliminate fiscal drag, and move the economy toward full employment.

Budget outlays for national defense did increase over $3.6 billion in fiscal year 1962, by over $1 billion in the next two years, and combined with increases in outlays on welfare and Social Security provided temporary stimulus to the economy. The full employment surplus fell to $9 billion, and the gap between potential and actual output fell by $15 billion (1958 prices).

This government stimulus was not sufficient as the private sector failed to respond with increased spending, and the output gap rose again to the $25–30 billion range (1958 prices). Long-run tax initiatives, the investment tax credit, and accelerated depreciation allowances designed to encourage private spending on capital goods enacted in 1962 did not affect the immediate situation. The Kennedy administration began to advocate another tax reduction, but was unable to convince Congress as to its necessity. That task was left to the Johnson administration.

No doubt the military spending stimulus helped to reduce the slack in the economy. Moreover this conclusion is based on a rather narrow definition of defense spending. If other areas of expenditure that are connected to national defense, such as space and technology, international affairs, veterans' payments, atomic energy research, and interest costs, are added to the defense bill, the economic impact is enlarged substantially.

For example, federal government *purchases* of national defense items as a percentage of all of its purchases on goods and services is one widely used measure of the impact of defense spending on the economy. In the years 1961, 1962, and 1963, these percentages were 83.3, 81.4, and 79.1 respectively. These amounts do not include the portion on military affairs that can be alloted to spending on atomic energy or space research and development. By any standard, defense spending was an important ingredient in eliminating the slack in the economy in this period. Finally the costs of the defense buildup do not include funds spent by the CIA in pursuit of its objectives. As always the amounts spent by the CIA are not made public, and this usually results in an understatement of defense spending.

But the impetus for national defense spending was not the Vietnam problem but the result of the policy designed to close the alleged missile gap between the Soviet Union and the United States. The amounts spent in Vietnam up to 1965 of less then $700 million, excluding foreign aid, are not likely to have played a significant role in affecting the U.S. economy. By themselves, expenditures on Vietnam were just too small at this stage.

Perhaps as important as the actual defense outlays was the preparation by the Kennedy administration for additional defense outlays in the future. Aside from the buildup in missiles to close a nonexistent gap, there were other incidents that prepared the public for more defense spending: the response to the Russian threat to deny Western access to East Berlin; the Bay of Pigs operation, the invasion of Cuba by CIA directed forces; the Russian construction of missile sites in Cuba; the space program that promised to land men on the moon by the end of the decade; and of course, the whole Southeast Asia problem, including the problems in Laos. All of these episodes created an atmosphere of distrust and hostility and consequently created the fear necessary to justify the expenditures on defense. The cold war continued, in short, and soon a hot one would emerge.

Whether the course of history would have been significantly altered had Kennedy lived is problematic; his private ambivalence about U.S. involvement was matched by his public belligerence. This is understandable given the muddled reports and forecasts he was receiving, but whether he would have withdrawn from Southeast Asia, as he indicated he would if he got a second term, is far from certain.

NOTES

1. Stanley Karnow, *Vietnam: A History* (New York: Viking Press, 1983), 197–98. This is an excellent source for the history and development of U.S. involvement in Southeast Asia. See also Neil Sheehan, *A Bright Shining Lie* (New York: Random House, 1988), for a detailed account of the early days of the military war and the Vietnamese society and the subsequent military buildup and the society's deterioration.

2. Ibid., 20.

3. Department of Defense, *Semiannual Report of the Secretary of Defense, January 1 to June 30, 1954* (Washington, D.C.: U.S. Government Printing Office, 1955), 56. Also quoted in Major Generâl Leonard B. Taylor, *Financial Management of the Vietnam Conflict, 1962–1972* (Washington, D.C: Department of the Army, 1974), 16.

4. This is better known as the Food for Peace program. It was designed to insure the stability of American agriculture while at the same time improving the foreign relations of the United States. Under the program, U.S. food was sold at easy credit terms, payable in local currencies. Billed as a humanitarian program, the actual effects were often perverse, as the sought after markets for U.S. food forced out local farmers when prices fell, and altered food tastes in favor of U.S. crops and American eating habits.

5. U.S. House of Representatives, Committee on Appropriations, *Department of Defense Appropriations for 1967*, Part 1, 378. A complete table of armed forces involved to 1966 can be found in Murray L. Weidenbaum, *Economic Impact of the Vietnam War*, Center for Strategic Studies, Special Report Series No. 5 (Georgetown University, Washington, D.C.: Renaissance Editions, 1967), 4.

6. Wiedenbaum, *Economic Impact*, 21.

7. U.S. Congress, Joint Economic Committee, *Economic Effect of Vietnam Spending*, 90th Congress, 1st session (1967), 1:26.

8. Murray Weidenbaum has been instrumental in calling attention to these problems. For an example see his *Economic Impact*, 11–17. The timing of government spending on national defense will be the subject of more importance in Chapter 2.

9. Richard N. Goodwin, *Remembering America: A Voice from the Sixties* (Boston: Little, Brown, 1988), 372. The parenthesis in the quote is concluded by the damaging comparison:

> But military men, like economists, are easily seduced by the security of statistics and, invariably, when the numbers don't "work" (i.e., halt or defeat the enemy), simply change their "quantitative estimates" without challenging the assumptions on which error was built, a technique that may be useful in the war games room of the Pentagon but is not so serviceable in a real war.

10. See Karnow, *Vietnam: A History*, for the record of gradual buildup in Vietnam and James L. Clayton, *The Economic Impact of the Cold War* (New York: Harcourt, Brace & World, 1970), 44, Table 13 for the estimated cost of personnel and their support.

11. Quoted in Karnow, *Vietnam: A History*, 253.

12. These estimates were taken from the *Economic Report of the President, 1968*, 65–66.

2 THE ECONOMY PRIOR TO FULL-SCALE WAR

Lyndon Baines Johnson was sworn in as president on the same day that Kennedy was assassinated, November 22, 1963. A complex personality, Johnson has been called the consummate politician, at times proud then humble, manipulative then submissive, kind then vicious, and so on, but no list of adjectives could capture this larger than life Texan. From those who knew him, any or all of these adjectives would fit this moody man: kind, cruel, loud, gentle, coarse, bold, blunt, shrewd, intelligent, and feisty.

His critics however were quick to point out his relative ignorance about foreign affairs. Whether or not the charge was true need not concern us, but that was the perception since his days as Majority Leader of the Senate. However one example may serve to illustrate how this complex man operated. Sent to Vietnam by Kennedy, Johnson repeated the domino theory and in a rhetorical flourish compared South Vietnam's President Ngo Dinh Diem to Winston Churchill only later to admit "Diem's the only boy we got out there."[1] Here political rhetoric is matched by pragmatism, but he never condoned efforts to overthrow Diem who was later assassinated in a coup.

Now he was president and must make the crucial decisions in a deteriorating situation in South Vietnam. Feeling vaguely illegitimate[2] and being untested, he turned to his secretary of defense, Robert McNamara for counsel and eventually to the Joint Chiefs of Staff. The Chiefs advocated widening the war as the current antiguerrilla tactics were clearly not working, and the war would have to be carried to the North.[3] After Johnson won the election of 1964, he was ready to commit U.S. troops and whatever else was necessary to rescue the situation and prevent a communist takeover of South Vietnam. Rejecting appeasement and fearing the right wing reaction to the loss of South Vietnam to the communists, Johnson was caught between a rock and a hard place, as his fellow Texans would put it. In a much quoted admission made to Doris Kearns, he put it bluntly:

> If I left the woman I really loved—the Great Society—in order to get involved with that bitch of a war on the other side of the world, then I would lose everything at home. All my programs. All my hopes to feed the hungry and shelter the homeless. All my dreams to provide education and medical care to the browns and the blacks and the lame and the poor. But if I left that war and let the communists take over South Vietnam, then I would be seen as a coward and my nation would be seen as an appeaser and we would both find it impossible to accomplish anything for anybody anywhere on the entire globe.[4]

True these words were spoken in retrospect, but there is little doubt that they reflect the anguish of the new president as he sanctioned the relentless escalation of the Vietnam conflict and U.S. involvement in it.

THE ECONOMIC SITUATION

The economic consequences of Johnson's desire to protect his Great Society programs while fending off communism were to be considerable and were thought so at the time. Before outlining them, however, it is necessary to take a closer look at the economy prior to the decisions to escalate U.S. participation.

The economy recovered in the first year of the Kennedy administration largely through the efforts of fiscal policy. Government purchases increased by 9 percent, and private investment rose by 30 percent. Prices remained stable with the Consumer Price Index (CPI) increasing by only 1.1 percent in 1961. Unemployment, however, remained high, at 6.1 percent in December. The administration, unhappy with so high a rate, set a target rate of 4 percent for its definition of full employment.

Although the gap between potential and actual GNP was closing, the administration economists, led by Walter Heller as chairman of the Council of Economic Advisors, began to worry over the problem of fiscal drag; the problem that occurs when tax receipts rise in a recovery period, which if not spent, would hinder the growth of the economy and prevent it from reaching its potential. So Walter Heller began urging a tax cut to alleviate the problem and keep the economy growing.[5] This Keynesian fiscal policy was revolutionary in its time since conventional wisdom held that cutting taxes when the budget was already in deficit was fiscally irresponsible.

In fact, Heller did have considerable difficulty in explaining the rationale for this fiscal policy and in convincing the president of its efficacy. Eventually he succeeded, and when the economy faltered in mid-1962 and a recession appeared likely, tax cut proposals were initiated. Kennedy hesitated at first and settled for a mini tax bill that permitted firms to accelerate depreciation deductions and take an investment tax credit of 7 percent on new capital goods purchases. In January 1963, all doubts gone and the conversion to Keynesian economics complete, he submitted the tax measure favored by his Council of Economic Advisors.

The tax bill proposed reductions in both individual and corporate tax rates: individual rates would fall in stages from the range of 20–91 percent to 14–65 percent and reduce tax liabilities by $6 billion in 1963 with further reductions to come in 1964 and 1965; corporate rates would also fall in stages from 52 to 47 percent and reduce tax liabilities by $13.5 billion, when fully operational in 1965. The tax plan met with considerable resistance, however, and was not passed in Kennedy's last year in office. The economy was not responding, and as the year 1963 was coming to an end, the unemployment rate still hovered around 5.6 percent, and real GNP was growing at a 3.8 percent rate, down from the 6.1 percent rate of a year earlier. Prices remained stable signifying the amount of slack in the economy, and hence the Council was looking forward to action on the tax bill in 1964 to reduce the $30 billion gap between potential and actual GNP.

Here is where Johnson's skill as a politician became evident. Using his famous pressure techniques combined with the sympathy generated by Kennedy's assassination, he was able to get quick action on the stalled tax bill. In February the Revenue Act of 1964, the largest tax cut in history to that date, was signed into law. It provided for cuts in tax rates over two years leading to eventual reductions of tax liabilities of $11 billion for individuals as it lowered tax rates to the range of 14–70 percent, and $3 billion in reductions for corporations as their rates were reduced to 48 percent from 52 percent. The effects on the economy were quickly felt: withholding rates on wages and salaries were reduced immediately rather than in stages, and household disposable incomes were thus immediately available for spending. As these incomes were spent, and respent in working their way through the economy, the actual effect would be greater than the tax reductions. This "multiplier" effect meant that incomes increased by $9 billion in 1964 alone, with further increases to be expected in 1965 and beyond.[6] Hailed as a revolutionary fiscal policy by many and condemned by others, this Act has remained controversial ever since its passage.

One question that made it controversial was, and still is, did this fiscal policy work or did monetary policy really do the job?[7] The question, though intriguing, cannot be pursued here, and putting aside the debate, it is evident that one or both policies worked to stimulate the economy. Economic growth revived as real GNP grew by 5.5 percent in 1964, and by 6.3 percent in 1965; unemployment fell to 5.4 percent in December 1964, and to 4.4 percent in December of 1965, close to the target rate of 4 percent; prices were stable in 1964 with the GNP price index rising by 1.6 percent and the CPI by 1.3 percent; in 1965 prices began to rise midway through the year, and for the entire year there were increases of 2.2 percent for the GNP index and 1.7 percent for the CPI. The price increases were dismissed as not critical in 1965 as economists were delighted with the success of the Keynesian experiment. The tax cut eliminated the fiscal drag problem, and the economy performed exactly as predicted. "Thus the rationale of the 1964 tax-cut proposal came straight out of the country's postwar textbooks," wrote Heller.[8]

Yet the above numbers do not isolate the effects of the tax cut and do not prove that the tax cut actually was responsible for the improvements in the economy. What would have happened to the economy had the tax cut not been enacted? Such questions are always difficult to answer since it is impossible to hold the world constant while examining a particular policy. However with large-scale econometric models that attempt to replicate the structure of the economy and given suitable assumptions about the path of the economy without the policy being considered, it is possible to simulate how the economy might have behaved. Then the actual history of the economy can be compared to the simulated "neutral" world with neutral fiscal and monetary policies.

Two such studies were conducted for the Joint Economic Committee by the Data Resources Inc. (DRI) and the Wharton Econometric Forecasting Associates (WEFA). Their conclusions on the effectiveness of the 1964 tax cut are similar: it increased real GNP by 0.8 percent in 1964 and between 1.3 and 1.6 percent in 1965 and 1966; it had virtually no effect on the GNP price index in 1964 and then raised it to .03 to .05 percent in 1965 and 1966; finally it reduced the unemployment rate by a range of 0.2 to 0.4 percent in 1964 and an additional 0.2 to 0.5 percent in 1966.[9] The numbers, of course, are merely estimates and their methodology open to criticism. Still if they are at all indicative of the real impact of the 1964 tax cut, they indicate the effectiveness of that policy and of fiscal policy in general.

THE INTRUDING WAR

Johnson had wanted desperately to win the presidency in his own name and devoted a great deal of his attention to that end. But the war in Asia would not go away and about all he could do publicly was to promise that American troops would not be fighting for Asian boys in their war. Conveniently Barry Goldwater, the Republican nominee for the presidency, agreed not to make Vietnam an issue in the campaign.[10]

Behind the scenes, however, the decisions on the future of U.S. involvement were being made in secret. The extent of the current involvement in Vietnam was also not publicized. U.S. military "advisors" were sent to Vietnam even before the French withdrawal. Their numbers grew slowly at first averaging approximately 700 up to 1960. After Kennedy took office, these advisors doubled to 1376 by December 1961, rose to 9865 by December 1962 and to 16,575 by December 1963. By December 1964, 23,300 advisors were in South Vietnam.

These military advisors were expected to train the South Vietnamese armed forces but not get involved themselves with the actual fighting. Gradually this prohibition broke down, as the South Vietnamese proved to be reluctant to take advice and even more to fight. As a result, U.S. military personnel became more and more involved in the actual conduct of the war. These actions were often concealed from high ranking U.S. military personnel, and from visiting officials who were checking on the progress of the South Vietnamese development. Meanwhile, the CIA was busy manipulating the political structure of the South Vietnamese government to make it conform to U.S. interests. In short, the United States was heavily involved in the internal affairs of the South Vietnamese government and was slowly taking over the military operations as well. The air force was busy bombing suspected "communist" hamlets in South Vietnam, thus creating potential converts to the Vietcong, while the CIA was busy forging a government more to U.S. liking.[11]

Over the years, officials in Washington, including the presidents, were supplied false reports, erroneous accounts of conditions on and off the battlefield, conflicting forecasts of military and political successes, contrasting views on how to proceed, and misconceptions of all kinds about the people of Southeast Asia. After much vacillation over how and when to proceed, some determination of the South Vietnamese problem had to be made. It came following McNamara's visit to Vietnam in the spring of 1964; the decision was made to increase support to the South Vietnamese. There were plans to bomb the strategic targets in the North and to blockade the harbor at Haiphong. But these acts would require a declaration of war, and lacking congressional support, that had to be avoided. A congressional "resolution", authorizing the president to act as if there were a war would do just as well, and such a resolution, which had been suggested by W. W. Rostow of the State Department, was drafted in May by William Bundy, also in the State Department.

All that was needed now was an excuse to invoke such a resolution for Congress would surely act if U.S. ships or troops were in peril. The incident that precipitated the adoption of such a resolution finally did occur in the Tonkin Gulf and gave the resolution its name. In early August two U.S. destroyers were acting as bait in searching out newly installed radar installations in the gulf just eight miles from North Vietnamese shores. They were probably in violation of North Vietnamese territorial waters when they were allegedly attacked. There were two alleged attacks by the North Vietnamese: in the first instance, there was such confusion aboard the U.S. ships that what actually happened in the clashes between the North's torpedo boats and the U.S. Navy's destroyers was suspect; in the second case, there probably never was an attack at all, but Johnson ordered reprisals against the North and eagerly used the incidents to get congressional approval for the Tonkin Gulf Resolution that gave the president wide powers to "take all necessary measures" . . . "to prevent further aggression," etc. The House approved the resolution unanimously and only two senators, Wayne Morse (R.–Oreg.) and Earnest Gruening (D.–Alaska) voted nay on August 6, 1964. The constraints on U.S. actions were now removed, and without the need for subterfuge the escalation proceeded in earnest.

By December 31, 1964, the number of troops in South Vietnam had risen to 23,300 and by June 30, 1965 to 103,000; the increases continued until by December 31, 1965, the number had grown to 184,000 and by June 30, 1966, to 322,000. (See Table 3.1.) The numbers of troops attest to one form of escalation, but in addition the United States began bombing North Vietnam in February 1965, and the war was clearly becoming more obvious to the general public.

ECONOMIC DEVELOPMENTS

The war would have been less remote and generated more discussion had the costs been made clear, or the effects had been quickly felt in a decline in economic well-being. As it was, no such painful effects were felt in the early stages of the war, and in fact while the military buildup was proceeding, the Great Society was flowering. Some of the Great

Society programs enacted or expanded in this period included: Federal aid to Appalachia, federal grants to education, and manpower programs were extended and expanded; Medicare was passed, providing medical care insurance to the aged, and at the same time Social Security benefits were increased while Social Security taxes were raised; health-center grants to states were enacted, and community health services were extended; a housing program for low-income families was passed; grants were made for water and sewage facilities, for water and air pollution programs, and for medical school construction; scholarships and libraries were authorized, and loan guarantees for needy students were established. Thus billions of dollars were being spent or authorized at the same time that the military buildup was occurring.

Meanwhile a *reduction* in excise taxes was passed in June 1965 that would have reduced taxes by $1.75 billion at annual rates (the measure was reversed in March 1966), and the first supplemental budget increase for fiscal year 1965 of $700 million for the Vietnam war was passed in May 1965. Together with the Great Society spending and the increased military expenditures, these measures should have called for some modifications of the forecasts for the economy in the latter half of 1965 and beyond.

The trouble was that economists did not see the military buildup in the data they normally examine to chart the course of the economy. As mentioned earlier, there are lags between the time that military orders are placed and when they are delivered and paid for. After military orders are placed, or obligated in technical terms, private defense contractors begin to produce the goods or services, and their payments for wages, rents, interests, and profits, begin to affect the economy directly and are recorded in the GNP. When these goods are later delivered to the government, the economic impact has already been felt in the economy—too late to register the true timing of the economic effects.[12] If the lags between orders and delivery are long (and they surely are variable depending on the type of good or service) the economic impact of military spending may be misjudged by considerable periods.

According to Weidenbaum the military buildup in 1965 was one such period when the impact was missed.[13] Defense expenditures on a fiscal year basis show a decline of $4.1 billion from 1964 to 1965 and then show an increase to fiscal year 1966 of $7.5 billion. Thus it would appear that defense expenditures affected the economy in fiscal year 1966. However, looking at quarterly data of defense expenditures on a calendar year basis reveals that the increase occurred in the fourth quarter of 1965 by $3.8 billion.

Yet defense obligations, the orders for goods or contracts placed, show the increase to have occurred in the second quarter of 1965, and as can be seen in Table 2.1, such obligations are greater than actual expenditures in the official accounts. Clearly the impact on the economy was felt earlier than was recognized, and the buildup was stronger than realized at the time. This point is made by Arthur Okun, who became the chairman of the Council of Economic Advisors under Johnson, when he admitted that economic forecasts were deficient because of the underestimation of defense activity in this period.[14]

Unfortunately the difficulty of measuring the impact of defense activity is not confined to this period. Even after noting the differences between obligations and expenditures, there remains the problem that spending out of obligations is also not smooth or predictable. Obligations for a major weapons system could be incurred in one period and actual economic activity could occur in another, or partial payments could be made, or postponements

Table 2.1
U.S. Defense Obligations and Expenditures (Billions of Dollars at Annual Rates and Seasonally Adjusted)

Calendar Year		Defense Obligations	Defense Expenditures (GNP basis)
1964	I	55.2	51.2
	II	54.8	50.9
	III	53.3	50.3
	IV	53.3	49.4
	Total	54.2	50.4
1965	I	51.0	48.6
	II	55.0	49.7
	III	59.0	50.9
	IV	62.1	54.7
	Total	56.8	51.0
1966	I	64.6	56.8
	II	75.9	60.1
	III	75.2	64.4
	IV	72.9	66.8
	Total	72.0	62.0

Source: For obligations, Murray L. Weidenbaum, *Economic Impact of the Vietnam War*, Center for Strategic Studies (Georgetown University, Washington, D.C.: Renaissance Editions, 1967), 23; for expenditures, Department of Commerce, Bureau of Economic Analysis, *The National Income and Product Accounts of the United States, 1929–82* (Washington, D.C.: U.S. Government Printing Office, 1986), Table 3.2.

could follow, or outright cancellations could be made. Thus the detailed data necessary to attempt an impact analysis are not available, or if available would require an enormous amount of study to reveal the actual impact.

The gain in accuracy may be worth the effort in some cases, but in the general type of historical overview undertaken here, the loss in correctly identifying the precise period when defense spending affected the economy is not that critical. It would be most important to those who are responsible for formulating current economic policy for it would be critical to know how the economy will be affected in the near future for timely actions to be taken.

Since we are examining the past, there is no sense of urgency in learning the exact timing pattern of defense activity.[15] Nevertheless, an attempt was made to analyze the problem in order to understand how serious the problem really was and whether or not it had a serious effect on the formation of policy in the period under investigation. A cursory examination does reveal the existence of a lag of one to two quarters from obligations to expenditures, but the lag is not consistent nor uniform; without further study it is impossible to state with any confidence either the nature of the lag or its effect on policy formation.[16]

In other areas of the economy, the voluntary wage-price guideposts, inaugurated under the Kennedy administration, were challenged by the steel producers in November 1965, and even more aggressively by aluminum producers. The wage settlements in both of these key industries were very important to the efforts toward price stabilization.

The guidepost program was designed to teach labor and management (and the public) about the fundamental relationships among productivity, costs, and prices. If wage increases matched productivity increases, costs would be constant, and hence price increases (inflation) could be held constant while the distribution of income between labor and other factors of production would remain constant, thereby benefiting all sides and eliminating the fighting over productivity gains. The guidepost program was designed to combat inflation brought about by workers demanding wage increases in excess of the growth of labor productivity, thus increasing unit labor costs and eventually prices. In areas characterized by market power, where the guideposts were targeted, the increased labor costs could be passed on in the form of higher prices. What was thought needed at the time was an educational program that would inform both workers and firms of the benefits of limiting their demands to what the growth of productivity warranted. The Council of Economic Advisors noted that if wages were to increase in line with the average growth in labor productivity, at that time 3.2 percent, then both costs and prices need not increase.

In industries where the growth in labor productivity increased by more than 3.2 percent, prices should have a tendency to fall, and the reverse where the growth in labor productivity was less than 3.2 percent. (This was a long-run program, where the changes in prices and behavior could be smoothly accomplished; it is, however, often viewed as a year to year guide to wage and price changes).[17]

In both the aluminum and steel cases, producers had raised prices above the noninflationary limits set by the voluntary guidelines. In the aluminum case, the producers rescinded the increase (after the administration threatened to sell aluminum from its stockpile), but in the steel case, government purchases from lower priced steel producers only resulted in limiting the price rise rather than halting it. These major challenges to the voluntary guideposts would make them increasingly vulnerable until they collapsed entirely in 1966.

In December 1965 the federal government began to experience friction between monetary and fiscal policy makers. The Federal Reserve, under Chairman William M. Martin, decided to increase the discount rate to 4.5 percent from 4 percent in its effort to control inflation. (In June, Chairman Martin made a speech that sent shivers throughout the economy when he said that he found "disquieting similarities" between the present state of the economy and that of the 1920s just prior to the depression.) The executive branch complained and felt the raising of the discount rate was unwarranted at this time and in any case, should have been undertaken only when properly coordinated with fiscal policy, now being formulated. In retrospect the Federal Reserve was correct to worry about inflation as was later admitted by Arthur Okun: " To administration economists, this [raising of the discount rate] seemed debatable at the time the decision was being made by the Fed; but once the plant and equipment survey was in front of them, they recognized that the Fed was right on that score."[18]

NOTES

1. The response is to the question by Stanley Karnow of whether he meant to make such a comparison. See Stanley Karnow, *Vietnam* (New York: Viking Press, 1983), 214.

2. He told his biographer Doris Kearns, "I took the oath. I became President. But for millions of Americans I was still illegitimate, a naked man with no presidential covering, a pretender to the throne, an illegal usurper." See Doris Kearns, *Lyndon Johnson and the American Dream.* (New York: Harper & Row, 1976), 170.

3. For another excellent history of the Vietnam involvement see, David Halberstam, *The Best and the Brightest* (New York: Random House, 1972). Reprinted by Fawcett

Publications of Greenwich, Connecticut in 1973. Chapters 17 and 18 detail the events of the early Johnson administration.

4. Kearns, *Lyndon Johnson*, 251–52.

5. Heller outlined the economic problem and the political problem of educating the president on the need for a tax cut when the economy was already experiencing a deficit in his highly readable book, Walter W. Heller, *New Dimensions in Political Economy* (New York: W. W. Norton, 1967).

6. See the *Economic Report of the President, 1965*, 65.

7. For more on the debate over the tax cut, see Milton Friedman and Walter W. Heller, *Monetary vs. Fiscal Policy* (New York: Norton, 1969).

8. Heller, *New Dimensions in Political Economy*, 72.

9. U.S. House of Representatives, Committee on the Budget, Joint Economic Committee, 95th Congress, 2nd session, *Economic Stabilization Policies: The Historical Record, 1962–76* (Washington, D.C.: U.S. Government Printing Office, 1978), 8. For other studies that are consistent with the results of these studies see Arthur M. Okun, "Measuring the Impact of the 1964 Tax Cut," in *Readings in Money, National Income, and Stabilization Policy*, edited by Warren L. Smith and Ronald L. Teigen, 345–58 (Homewood, Ill.: Richard D. Irwin, 1970); and Lawrence R. Klein, "Econometric Analysis of the Tax Cut of 1964," in *The Brookings Model: Some Further Results*, edited by J. S. Duesenberry et al., 459–72 (Chicago: Rand McNally, 1969).

10. Barry M. Goldwater, *With No Apologies* (New York: Morrow, 1979), 75.

11. For a fascinating account of these early years of involvement, and for that matter of the Vietnam experience in general, see Neil Sheehan, *A Bright Shining Lie: John Paul Vann and America in Vietnam* (New York: Random House, 1988).

12. Perhaps a simple table would clarify the entire process. Murray Weidenbaum has outlined the spending process in many studies, and Table 2.2 is adapted from one of these. The table is overly simplified, of course, but the timing problem is clearly evident.

Table 2.2
Impact of the Military Procurement Process ($10 Billion Program)

Stage	Government Purchases	Business Inventories	GNP
1. Appropriation	–	–	–
2. Contract	–	–	–
3. Production	–	+10	+10
4. Delivery	+10	–10	–

Source: Adapted from M. L. Weidenbaum, *Economic Impact of the Vietnam War*.

13. Murray L. Weidenbaum, *Economic Impact of the Vietnam War*, Center for Strategic Studies (Georgetown University, Washington, D.C.: Renaissance Editions, 1967), 21–24. See also his background paper submitted to the Joint Economic Committee, "Impact of Vietnam War on American Economy," in *Economic Effects of Vietnam Spending*, U.S. Congress, 90th Congress, 1st session (Washington, D.C.: U.S. Government Printing Office, 1967), 1:193–215. For a further discussion of this problem and of the 1965 period in particular see Robert Warren Stevens, *Vain Hopes, Grim Realities* (New York: New Viewpoints, 1976), 67–73.

14. Arthur M. Okun, *The Political Economy of Prosperity* (New York: Norton, 1970), 67–68.

15. For a good description of the whole problem and possible solutions see Murray L. Weidenbaum, "The Economic Impact of the Government Spending Process," Congress of the United States, Joint Economic Committee, *Economic Effects of Vietnam Spending*, 90th Congress, 1st session (Washington, D.C.: U.S. Government Printing Office, 1967), 2:603–661.

16. Weidenbaum makes a similar lament, and also cites Arthur F. Burns and Paul W. McCracken, both past chairmen of the Council of Economic Advisors, who worried about the lack of data on the timely impact of government receipts and expenditures. See Weidenbaum, *Economic Impact*, 17 and his analysis of military data in the appendix. In another paper, "The Economic Impact of the Government Spending Process," Weidenbaum complicates the simple model cited above and shows that consumers and firms may react to the awarding of contracts before any production occurs. This so called "announcement effect" could be important in the effects on the economy. He also gives examples of the lag times between the letting of contracts and their delivery: from ½ year for military uniforms to 2¼ years for bombers and jet fighters. See the U.S. Congress, Joint Economic Committee, *Economic Effects of Vietnam Spending*, 90th Congress, 1st session (April 1967): 1:603–61. In the same source, Edward Greenberg's paper, "Employment Impacts of Defense Expenditures and Obligations" (663–77), does indeed find the lag in obligations to be important in explaining the changes in employment in aerospace industries.

These studies show how complicated the entire matter is, and although their results cannot be generalized and used in this book, they do verify the importance of lags in the military procurement process and the problem caused thereby for macroeconomic policy makers.

17. See the *Economic Report of the President 1967*, 120–127, for a review of the guidepost program, and the worry over its effectiveness in the coming years. For those confused by the arithmetic of the guideposts, here is the example given by the Council of Economic Advisors: If a worker in a particular firm is paid $2 an hour—$80 a week—and contributes to the production of 200 units a week, output per man-hour is 5 units (200 units divided by 40 hours), and unit labor cost is $.40 ($80 divided by 200 units). If, for whatever reason, output rises by 3 percent to 206 units a week—with no extra labor time required—output per man-hour is also up 3 percent, to 5.15 units (206 divided by 40 man-hours). If the wage rate also rises by 3 percent, to $2.06 an hour ($82.40 a week), unit labor costs will remain at $.40 ($82.40 divided by 206 units). If the price of the product is unchanged, the margin between price and unit labor cost—available to pay for others' contributions to production—will be the same. But with 3 percent more

units sold, the total amount available to pay others, including owners, will also rise by 3 percent.

18. Okun, *The Political Economy of Prosperity*, 69.

II The War Years: The Economic Record

3 THE MIDDLE YEARS AND THE END OF THE JOHNSON ADMINISTRATION, 1966–68

By 1965 President Johnson had taken the United States a long way away from the pledge he had made much earlier, "We are not about to send American boys nine or ten thousand miles away from home to do what Asian boys ought to be doing for themselves." Now the United States was bombing North Vietnam and protecting our airfield at Danang with more and more troops; then inevitably more troops were needed to maintain logistical support, and so on, until by the end of 1965, nearly 200,000 troops were involved in South Vietnam. In the years to come, the same story would be told by General William Westmoreland, commander in chief of the armed forces until 1968: send more military personnel, and we can get the job done. The troop buildup in the middle years grew to over 536,000. Table 3.1 shows the dramatic increase. Of course tons of supplies, weapons, and materiel poured into South Vietnam as well to support the troops in the field. By now the strategy to win the war was divided into three components: the "search and destroy" operation whereby U.S. troops, using their superior firepower, would wear down the enemy; the bombing of the North; and the "pacification" program that was to help control the civilian population through economic and social means. Victory would be swift and relatively easy.

It did not work out that way. The search and destroy missions did not go smoothly and required the destruction of many villages. This inane policy is best illustrated by this ludicrous statement of an unnamed Army major who declared, "It became necessary to destroy the town to save it." (The town was Bentre, South Vietnam, population 35,000.) The bombing and defoliation of South Vietnam created thousands of refugees and worked counter to the stated pacification program. The bombing of the

Table 3.1
U.S. Military Personnel in Vietnam

Year (at Dec. 31)	Number
1965	184,314
1966	385,300
1967	485,600[1]
1968	536,100
1969	543,400[2]

1. Data do not include 76,500 men in Thailand or off-shore in 1967 and 1968. See James L. Clayton, ed., *The Economic Impact of the Cold War* (New York: Harcourt, Brace & World, 1970), 45.
2. Peak strength as of April 30, 1969.

Source: Department of Defense, *Selected Manpower Statistics* (Washington, D.C.: U.S. Government Printing Office, April 1971), 58.

North did not weaken the resolve of the North Vietnamese but in fact reinforced their determination. Nevertheless it was possible to believe, as did our military leaders, that the war of attrition would still be won, and indeed the war settled down to a grinding, routine struggle.

Dissent over the war was increasing every year as the escalation was underway, but the promise of early victory gave many the justification for reserving judgment. The domestic impact will be discussed later, but everyone's complacency was shattered when on January 31, 1968, the lunar new year or Tet observed by the Vietnamese, the communists launched a major offensive attacking 100 cities and towns, including Saigon the capital of South Vietnam. The Tet offensive demolished all thoughts that this would be a short war, easily won by superior U.S. forces that a backward country could hardly resist for very long. The character of the war changed from skirmishes in the jungles and rural villages to the urban streets and towns, the areas that were seemingly protected from attack. While it is true that Johnson's popularity had been declining prior to Tet, it was this reversal of U.S. plans, and this refutation of U.S. pronouncements about the war that led Johnson to revise his perceptions of the war and eventually helped to convince him to retire from political life.[1]

THE DOMESTIC SCENE

The war had never been explained nor justified to the American people. As a result whatever national unity existed beforehand quickly evaporated, and the nation quickly became sharply divided. No amount of falling dominoes convinced those who felt the war was unjust and unwarranted on the one side and on the other side, no amount of protests and dissent were sufficient to alter the anticommunist sentiment. The foreign policy in Southeast Asia became the major issue of the administration, and as it did so the discussions over its efficacy and morality generated increasing discussion, much of it rancorous, acrimonious, emotional, and harsh. The war became a cancer, eating away at the tissue that held society together.

All this was fueled by daily broadcasts of the war on television, and everyone, opponent and advocate alike, could watch the war in the fields and listen to interviews with the troops while eating dinner or waiting for more entertaining fare to begin. While the war was made immediate in our homes, many continued to maintain that it was nevertheless remote and unconnected to our own security; others reacted by insisting that even more military might be exerted, even nuclear weapons if necessary, to win at all costs. Reconciliation or even a reasoned dialogue between the two extremes was, and perhaps still is, impossible.

A good part of the intellectual establishment began to abandon Johnson and his war—the educational leaders, the college students, who were exempt from the draft in a shrewd move by Johnson not to alienate the middle class taxpayers, the clergy, and many business and community leaders. The educational establishment was the most vocal with student and faculty rallies, "teach-ins," marches, and demonstrations of all kinds, including the draft-card-burning rituals. By the end of 1967, positions had hardened and many began to prepare to defeat the president at the polls the next year.

The students rallied behind their antiwar hero, Democratic Senator Eugene McCarthy of Minnesota, who managed, with their help, a surprising showing in the New Hampshire primary in March. Encouraged by the results, Robert Kennedy decided to enter the race as well. Having considered the issue for some time, President Johnson announced a bombing halt on March 31, 1968, and after acknowledging a divided America, surprised everyone with this announcement, "With America's sons in the fields far away, with America's future under challenge right here at home. . . I do not believe that I should devote an hour a day of my time to any personal partisan causes. . . . Accordingly, I shall not seek, and will not accept, the nomination of my party for another term as your President."

America was indeed under challenge at home: Robert Kennedy was assassinated as was Martin Luther King; college campuses were in turmoil; blacks were rioting in the ghettoes of Watts, Newark, and Detroit in the first signs of the clash between promises and reality as the other war, on poverty, was also being lost. All these strands would coalesce at the Democratic convention in Chicago as the nation witnessed the clash of various elements of dissenting groups with the Chicago police in the streets outside convention headquarters. The Democratic candidate, Vice President Hubert Humphrey, unable or unwilling to disavow the war in Vietnam, fell victim to this domestic turmoil and eventually suffered at the polls as Richard Nixon, the Republican nominee, won a very narrow victory in November.

THE ECONOMY FOLLOWING THE BUILDUP

In his budget message accompanying the fiscal 1966 budget, Johnson wrote, "It is a budget of both opportunity and sacrifice. It begins to grasp the opportunities of the Great Society. It is restrained by the sacrifices we must continue to make in order to keep our defenses strong and flexible." A year later, in the fiscal 1967 budget we find, "we are determined to press confidently forward toward the· great Society—but we shall do so in an orderly and responsible way, and at a pace which reflects the claims of our commitments in Southeast Asia upon the Nation's resources . . . [for] it would be folly to present a budget which inadequately provided for the military and economic costs of sustaining our forces in Vietnam." The shift in emphasis is obvious as the Great Society had to be shortchanged as the war escalated. In Johnson's words again, "I was bound to be crucified either way I moved."[2]

Mr. Johnson's dilemma was eventually resolved in favor of guns not butter. There was no longer talk of providing both. In the 1966 budget, Johnson seemed to imply that the United States would and could meet its military needs to pursue its ends in Vietnam. However what was not stated in the budget was an assumption made by Secretary of Defense Robert McNamara that the war would be over by June 30, 1967. Thus requests for funds for Southeast Asia were made on the unannounced assumption that the conflict would require no additional funds for combat operations after June 30, 1967, and if that assumption were to prove false, supplementary funds would be necessary. The reason McNamara gave for his actions was to avoid the unnecessary production and stockpiling of military equipment that was the experience at the conclusion of the Korean War.

Yet this rather arbitrary assumption was to have severe consequences on the economy. The underestimation of expenditures necessary to continue the war meant that no provision for additional military expenditures was made in the budget, and furthermore no alterations were made in planned monetary or fiscal policies either. As a result there were no budgetary anticipation of nor provisions for the subsequent increases in spending that the prolongation of the war would require. Table 3.2 vividly illustrates the problem. Table 3.2 includes the original estimate of defense spending in Vietnam as well as the revised estimate of expenditures in a later budget; also included are the actual expenditures made on two bases. The "full" expenditure costs include all costs associated with the conflict in Vietnam. Full costs include all personnel costs, support costs, equipment and supply costs, training and maintenance costs, and so on. Incremental costs include only those costs that can be assigned to the war exclusively. That is, some of the costs incurred in South Vietnam would have been spent anyway in the normal course of defense spending and are thus deducted from the full costs to arrive at incremental costs. For example some of the ammunition spent might have been used in training exercises, some of the soldiers were permanent members of the armed forces, and some of the fuel for jet planes might have been used in training or in other parts of the world, and so on. (Economists might refer to incremental costs as marginal or extra costs incurred in Vietnam.) In other words, incremental costs, once no longer incurred, could become available for spending on peacetime activities.

Now the consequences of McNamara's assumption of an early end to the war can easily be seen. The expenditures for fiscal year 1967 were

Table 3.2
Estimated and Actual Expenditures for the Vietnam War (Billions of Dollars)

Fiscal Year	Expenditures			
	Original estimate	Revised estimate	Actual	
			Full Costs	Incremental Costs
1965	0.1	0.1	0.1	0.1
1966	4.4	5.8	5.8	5.8
1967	10.2	19.4	20.1	18.4
1968	21.9	24.5	26.5	20.0
1969	25.8	28.8	28.8	21.5

Source: *The Budget of the United States Government* (Washington, D.C.: U.S. Government Printing Office, 1967), 73–75; 1968, 77; 1969, 83; and U.S. Department of Defense, U.S. Assistant Secretary of Defense (Comptroller), *The Economics of Defense Spending: A Look at the Realities* (Washington, D.C.: U.S. Government Printing Office, 1972), 149.

originally estimated at $10.2 billion but actual expenditures were running at twice that amount. Had there been a great deal of slack in the economy, this infusion of demand might have been welcomed, but as we shall see, the economy was growing nicely after the tax cut of 1964, and the increase in demand simply threw the economy off course, causing it to overheat. These general statements will be elaborated later, but it is possible to look back with Walter Heller,

> One wistfully concludes that, were it not for Vietnam, early 1966 would have found us comfortably contemplating the form and size of the fiscal dividend needed to keep us on the road to full employ-ment, rather than considering what further actions might be needed to ease the strain on our productive capacity and deal with the vexing and perplexing problem of inflation.[3]

Indeed the situation would grow worse in 1967 and in fact, the actual expenditures for Vietnam were consistently underestimated throughout the 1960s; Heller and others correctly saw the need for some restraint although in the early stages of the buildup, he hoped, again wistfully, that perhaps the economy could roll with the punches of Vietnam spending.

The Council of Economic Advisors, under Chairman Gardner Ackley, was not as sanguine as it advised Johnson on December 10, 1965, even before the major underestimation of the war's costs, that he could not have the Great Society, the war, and price stability unless there was a tax increase.[4] Johnson, however, listened to political rather than economic advice and rejected the Council's warning. There apparently was no sentiment for a tax increase in Congress, for it would have been labeled a war tax, and would have opened the whole conduct of the war to congres-sional debate. Edwin Dale, of the *New York Times* charged Johnson and members of his administration with acting irresponsibly when they real-ized that spending was running at rates much higher than provided for in the budget and did nothing about it; he labeled it (in retrospect) "the colossal inflation goof."[5]

It would be easy to condemn the administration in retrospect, but at the time there was much uncertainty over the duration and costs of the war. In the words of Arthur Okun, then a member and later chairman of the Council of Economic Advisors,

> This political reality should be clear in retrospect, especially in view of the antagonism to the surcharge in 1967–68. There was much less

reason for higher taxes to get a sympathetic hearing at the beginning of 1966. At that time, to the untrained eye, the economy seemed to be doing remarkably well. Anybody who wanted to slow things down was a killjoy. . . . All [the] unfavorable consequences of the boom were still forecasts rather than facts. . . . The economists in the administration watched with pain and frustration as fiscal policy veered off course. The new developments meant they were no longer calling the shots in fiscal policy.[6]

ECONOMIC CONDITIONS

It is now time to look more closely at the economic consequences of the war and the confusion over its costs. First it is necessary to recount the actual data about the economy during the period 1966–68, the remaining years of the Johnson administration. The data recorded in Table 3.3 are those that were available at the time and not the subsequent revised ones based on new definitions, new data, new procedures, and so on. The original data are relevant if the concern is to understand the economic responses to the economic conditions known at the time. (The revised data were not significantly different anyway.)

The data for 1966 begin to show the results of the military buildup. The economy was progressing nicely, according to the textbooks, wrote Walter Heller, when the increase in national defense was added to the spending stream without any offset in the way of restraint either from other expenditure areas of the budget or from increases in taxes. The GNP spurted by 8.5 percent in nominal dollars from 1965 to 1966 and by 5.4 percent in real terms or corrected for inflation. As might be expected, the unemployment rate dipped below 4 percent for the first time since the early 1950s as it fell to 3.9 percent for the year and to 3.8 percent in December. As spending increased manufacturers began to utilize more of their plant and equipment, and the rate of capacity usage rose to a relatively high 91 percent.

Thus the economy was utilizing more of its productive capacity with unemployment falling to below the full employment definition of 4 percent and with its plant and equipment reaching full capacity as well. Clearly the gap between potential and actual productive capacity was closed in 1966; potential GNP was growing at approximately 4 percent (man-hours were growing at 1.5 percent and labor productivity at 2.5 percent), and actual GNP was growing at 5.4 percent. But just as clearly, the actual rate of growth could not continue without running into labor shortages or

Table 3.3
Selected Economic Series, 1966–68 (Quarterly Data at Annual Rates)

Cal. Year & Quarter	GNP (bill) GNP	GNP (bill) National Defense Purchases	GNP (in 1958 $)	Unemploy Rate (%)	Prices CPI (1957-59=100) %Change	Prices WPI (1957-59=100) % Change	Prices GNP Index (1958=100) % Change	Mfg. Operating Capacity (%)
1966	739.5	60.0	647.7	3.9	2.9	3.2	3.0	91.0
1966 I	721.2	54.6	640.5	3.8	0.7	1.4	0.9	91.0
II	732.3	57.1	643.5	3.9	1.1	0.5	1.1	91.0
III	745.3	62.0	649.9	3.9	0.9	1.0	0.8	91.0
IV	759.1	65.5	657.0	3.8	0.8	-0.7	0.8	90.0
1967	785.1	72.6	669.2	3.8	2.8	0.2	3.0	85.1
1967 I	766.3	70.2	660.7	3.7	0.2	0.0	0.6	87.1
II	775.1	72.5	664.7	3.8	0.7	-0.2	0.5	84.9
III	791.2	73.3	672.0	3.9	1.0	0.5	0.9	84.1
IV	807.6	74.3	679.4	4.0	0.9	0.1	1.0	84.3
1968	860.7	78.9	706.9	3.6	4.0	2.5	3.8	84.4
1968 I	831.2	76.8	692.7	3.6	1.0	1.3	0.9	84.9
II	852.9	79.0	703.4	3.6	1.2	0.6	1.0	84.8
III	871.0	79.6	712.3	3.6	1.2	0.5	0.9	84.0
IV	887.8	80.0	719.1	3.4	1.1	0.5	1.0	84.1

Source: Economic Reports of the President, 1967–1969 (Washington, D.C.: Government Printing Office).

bottlenecks. The increase in demand could be met as long as there were idle resources, but now that full employment was being reached, the economy could grow only by its potential, or by its growth in productive capacity.[7]

As might be expected, the required growth could not take place in the short run which put pressure on the existing resources and of course on prices. Where the CPI was increasing at a rate of 1.6 percent in 1965, the rate now rose to 2.9 percent in 1966; the Wholesale Price Index (WPI) increased from a rate of 1.9 percent to 3.2 percent, and the GNP index increased from a rate of 1.8 percent to 3.0 percent in the same period. Inflation was an unwanted intruder in the economy, and the administration had no ready plan to deal with it; a tax increase was not proposed, wage and price controls were not considered, and the Great Society was still being sought.

However the tight labor market almost assured that the price increases would be reflected in wage demands, and wage demands would be reflected in higher prices. Thus average hourly compensation in the private nonfarm economy increased by 5.6 percent from 1965 to 1966 while labor productivity rose by a rate of only 2.4 percent giving rise to an increase in unit labor costs of 3.2 percent. Wage earners saw prices, especially of food and medical services rising, and despite the decline in the *rate* of growth of productivity, increased their demands for higher wages. One such demand destroyed the only restraint on wages in existence—the guideposts—that were introduced in the Kennedy administration whereby wage increases were supposed to be related to the rate of increase in labor productivity to avoid inflation. A midsummer strike by the airline machinists was settled by a wage increase far in excess of the wage guideposts still technically in existence in 1966. The rationale for the voluntary wage restraint of labor and the adherence to the old standard was disappearing now as prices (CPI) were rising at a rate of 3.3 percent while average labor productivity was rising at a rate of 2.4 percent. According to the "rules" prices should not be increasing, or if so by small amounts, since productivity was rising by greater rates than the average in many key industries. Hence profits were rising, and these were observed by organized labor, no friend of the guideposts anyway. The rising prices and profits furnished excuses, if they were needed, to press for higher wages. But if wage increases are greater than labor productivity increases, unit labor costs rise, giving an excuse for higher prices, etc. Since the guideposts were becoming irksome to both labor and firms, many of whom never were very cooperative, and since no particular sacrifice was demanded of either, the guidepost program collapsed. [8] Moral suasion has its limits and jawboning by the administration for restraint went unheeded.

Fiscal policy in this period was clearly inappropriate. With no real restraint on spending and no really effective tax increase, fiscal actions did not alleviate the excess demand pressures that were building. True, excise taxes on telephones and transportation were restored and withholding rates were graduated to "put them on a pay-as-you-go" basis and possibly some spending on nondefense was held down, but these actions were simply insufficient to cope with the problem. In September, however, the administration asked for a suspension of the investment tax credit, and it was granted in October. As a method of reducing the excess demand such a move could not be totally effective in a boom period and may have worked against the needed increase in productive capacity. If investment in capital goods was curtailed as a result of the tax change, then the additional supply of goods that the foregone investment might have produced would not be forthcoming to help reduce excess demand and moderate the pressure on prices.

The incorrect fiscal policy was quickly registered in the federal budgets. The deficit in the fiscal year budget for 1966 rose to $3.8 from $0.6 billion and the calendar year budget in the national income accounts rose to a deficit of $0.2 billion from a surplus of $1.2 billion. Finally the high employment budget also swung into a deficit of $3.6 billion from a surplus of $1.0 billion. This is the measure used to gauge the impact of government on the economy since it eliminates automatic government actions caused by the state of the economy, e.g. unemployment compensation payments, welfare payments, and so on. Clearly government was adding to the pressures on the economy by providing fiscal stimulus when some measure of restraint was required.

Lacking any real fiscal restraint, the burden of stabilization fell to the monetary authorities. The Federal Reserve reacted by letting the money supply, M1 (Demand deposits + currency outside banks), grow at less than 2 percent for the first half of the year, and then letting the rate fall to zero. With the economy booming, and the demand for funds high, while the supply of funds was restrained, something had to give. Banks scrambled around for funds, inventing new negotiable instruments, increasing interest rates to attract funds, bringing funds home from abroad, and borrowing funds from the Federal Reserve. Still the liquidity crisis continued with investment houses stuck with unsold security issues, states and localities unable to borrow to finance their activities, and thrift institutions losing funds to commercial banks.

The results were predictable. The housing market collapsed as its source of funds, the thrifts, were losing deposits and as interest rates increased dramatically. Mortgage interest rates were approaching 7 percent at year's end, a rate not seen in the post–World War II years. Of course housing starts fell, to 0.9 million units from 1.4 million, and the uneven effects of monetary policy were obvious to everyone. Meanwhile the Federal Reserve kept its discount rate at 4.5 percent letting banks borrow at this low rate and reloan at higher market rates. The rate on three month Treasury Bills, for example, rose to 5.4 percent in October from 4.6 percent in January before falling to 5.0 percent in December.

Apparently high interest rates did not deter investment spending in this period as the boom created expectations of even better future conditions.[9] Complaints against high interest rates were heard, but they were ignored in the name of fighting inflation. In the words of Okun, "the Federal Reserve's independence proved to be a valuable national asset. It permitted the President and his administration to assume a passive role, tolerating an unpopular tight money policy silently without explicitly approving or endorsing it."[10]

In the last quarter of 1966, the demand for funds eased somewhat as monetary policy showed its effectiveness. Some of the demand for funds fell off, the mortgage market was aided by an infusion of funds from the Federal National Mortgage Association, and the Federal Reserve aided the thrifts by reducing the maximum interest rate that could be paid on time deposits to 5 percent from 5.5 percent. Thus monetary policy proved effective, but its power was concentrated in a few areas, the housing market and small businesses. Moreover the effects of monetary policy on the distribution of income and wealth were detrimental to principles of equity. The incompatibility of an expansionary fiscal policy and a contractionary monetary policy was demonstrated in this period, and the consequences of their working at cross purposes were to have lasting effects on the economic and social system. Indeed in the next chapter, the case is made that the year 1966 was a pivotal one for the U.S. economy.

The credit crunch of 1966 frightened many people, and the administration and the Federal Reserve quickly reached an agreement to pull back from the stringent monetary policy. Toward the end of 1966 and throughout 1967, monetary policy moved toward ease with the money supply (M1) increasing about 6.5 percent over the year. Monetary policy became more accommodating to fiscal policy, for it was evident that using only monetary policy to control inflation had proved overly disrupting to financial and housing markets. The howls of these groups brought about the retreat from the tight monetary policy and the credit crunch.

Moreover the monetary policy of 1966, presumably designed to fight inflation, actually pushed the economy toward a recession and that eventuality became the primary concern. Inventories increased by 43 percent over 1965, business investment fell to zero growth from the previous 10 percent growth, and of course the housing market collapsed. According to Okun, the administration welcomed the slowdown because it offered a second chance to start over and remake the macroeconomic policy of 1966.[11] The Council of Economic Advisors was willing to accept the slowdown in the first half of the year if it were followed by the resumption of the expansion that began in 1961.

The economy did slow down in the first half of the year as the real rate of growth fell to 3.3 percent for the year, down from 5.4 percent. (See Table 3.3.) The unemployment rate was not affected very much as firms decided to retain or hoard their skilled workers even as their operating capacity fell to 85 percent from 91 percent in 1966. The average workweek fell instead as did the rate of growth of labor productivity, for the *rate* of growth of output was falling while employment remained stable. The growth of output per man-hour in nonfarm industries fell to 0.9 percent from 2.5 percent. Prices, however, continued to rise as the CPI and the GNP index rose by about 3 percent for the year. The fiscal response of the administration to these conditions was to ask for a reinstatement of the investment tax credit when the decline in investment spending became evident. The increase in idle productive capacity made this proposal seem insufficient to stem the fall in investment purchases, but the administration wanted to prevent a real collapse. Interestingly, the easy monetary policy did not seriously affect the nominal long-term rates of interest upon which investment plans might be influenced. In fact, interest rates began to rise slowly throughout the year, and since prices were rising as well, real interest rates (adjusted for inflation) were fairly constant. In April the Federal Reserve reduced its discount rate to 4 percent from 4.5 percent as part of its move toward monetary ease. Short-term interest rates fell by 1+ percentage points in the first half of the year but turned upward in the second half. However heavy borrowing by all sectors continued, perhaps spurred on by the fear of another credit crunch. The expectations of even higher future interest rates may have stimulated borrowing, even in the face of rising current interest rates. In any case the demand for funds was strong, and the composition of that demand was confusing.

The other major fiscal policy move of the administration was the request for a 6 percent surcharge on the tax liabilities of individuals and corporations effective July 1, 1967. With the economy in decline in the early part of 1967, the tax increase was not well received on Capitol Hill. Wilbur Mills, chairman of the House Ways and Means Committee, was not convinced of the need for a tax increase because there was no evidence of demand pull inflation, but there was evidence of supply inflation; inflation coming from the cost or supply side would not be affected by such a tax increase designed to affect the demand or spending side. Administration economists were not able to convince Congress or the American people of the need to enact a tax increase based upon forecasts of future economic conditions that might warrant such restraint. Unable or unwilling to identify the tax increase with patriotism and the war effort, the administration failed to get a tax bill passed in 1967.

The fall in interest rates did revitalize the housing market, and eventually the buildup in inventories was worked off. The economy started on the rebound in the latter half of the year. Finally in November, Great Britain devalued the pound in response to pressure from the international community. The United States was also under pressure to get its balance of payments in order, and the Federal Reserve reacted in the only way it could by increasing the discount rate back to 4.5 percent in order to protect the exchange rate of the dollar. International bankers were growing increasingly nervous with the chronic deficits in the U.S. balance of payments, and the shaky dollar, of which they had plenty, was forcing their hand. They began calling for reforms in the International Monetary Fund's rules. Thus international concerns were also impinging on the ability of the United States to conduct its monetary and fiscal policies.

Despite many forecasts to the contrary, the economic boom continued in 1968. The slowdown in 1967 was shorter than anticipated, and long-term expectations of prosperity soon overshadowed the short-term concern of a minor setback. Real GNP increased by 5.6 percent from 3.3 percent with all sectors of demand contributing. Investment spending rebounded, as did housing, and these increases took place despite interest rate increases caused by the return of monetary policy toward tightness. The behavior of investment spending in this period remains confusing and can be explained only if long-run profit expectations are introduced to cancel the short-run deterrents to investment demand. In other areas, the unemployment rate began to fall, and by November the rate was 3.3 percent. Prices, however, continued their inexorable rise as the CPI rose by 4.0 percent, the WPI by 2.5 percent and the GNP index by 3.8 percent. (See Table 3.3.)

The major fiscal policy move in this period was the passage of the temporary 10 percent tax surcharge in June 1968, made retroactive to April for individuals and to January for corporations. The surcharge was scheduled to end on June 30, 1969. Originally proposed in January 1967 as a 6 percent surcharge, it later increased to 10 percent and was finally passed a year and a half later. Consequently many suggested that the tax surcharge was too little and too late. Others suggested that it would not dampen demand since it would be regarded as temporary and consumers would continue their consumption plans since their plans are based on longer-run forecasts of their incomes. Since consumption did increase and saving fall, the view that the tax surcharge was ineffective must be given some credence. Others suggested that the increase in consumption would have been even greater without the tax surcharge, and therefore the tax was at least partially effective.[12]

As part of a deal that produced the tax surcharge, Congress forced the administration to cut back federal spending by $6 billion in nondefense areas. The administration was granted its military requests, but Congress exacted its price. The promise of guns and butter was broken. *The restraint came at the expense of social programs so that the disadvantaged in the United States would help pay for weapons to attack the less fortunate in a third world country.* When the surcharge was enacted, all talk of tax reform vanished, and again those who could not escape the tax surcharge would be the ones who would pay the tax.

The fiscal restraint for 1968 did not materialize in the first part of the year, and once enacted, did not work as effectively as hoped. Consequently monetary policy moved toward restraint in the first half of the year. The Federal Reserve raised the discount rate to a high of 5.5 percent in April and allowed the highest rate to be paid on large deposits under Regulation Q. The growth of the money supply slowed to 3.4 percent in the first half of the year and to 3 percent in the second half. Interest rates rose and surpassed those during the credit crunch of 1966. The demand for funds still exceeded the supply so that borrowing continued even as interest rates climbed. After the tax surcharge was passed, the Federal Reserve backed off somewhat as it reduced the discount rate to 5.25 percent, but interest rates still continued to rise until by the end of the year the three month Treasury bill was 5.9 percent, long-term rates were approaching 6 percent, and the Federal Housing Administration (FHA) mortgage rate was about 7.4 percent.

This very brief summary of the problems faced and the macroeconomic policies followed in the period 1965–68 has been supplied to provide some background of the economic conditions that were, at least in part, due to the involvement in Southeast Asia. It is not a complete record nor can all the economic conditions described be attributed to the Vietnam War. What emerges from the record is a rather confusing period for economists, and the macroeconomic policies followed reflect that confusion.[13] The record of both monetary and fiscal policy is not an exemplary one; monetary or fiscal policy worked at cross purposes or simply did not work at all. From the inappropriate fiscal policy as the war escalated to the stop-and-go monetary policy, macroeconomic policy-making in this period shows not only the political element in budget-making but also the confusion in prescribing for an economy that was overheating. It is not the purpose of this analysis to critique the macropolicies of the period, and these comments are made only in passing for now. Later their longer-term effects on the economic structure of the United States will be assessed.

Putting aside the evaluations of policy-making as the war intensified, it might be useful to pause and examine the changes in the economic structure that occurred in this period and specifically around the year 1966, i.e., at the start of the Vietnam escalation. These changes would affect the economy and the society for years after the conflict ended and are the overlooked economic consequences of the war in Southeast Asia.

WHAT IF THERE HAD BEEN NO WAR?

Before turning to these structural changes, however, it would be instructive to ask these questions: What if there had been no war? What would have happened to the U.S. economy?

These important questions have no simple answer, of course, but if they could be answered, we would gain some insight into the economic effects of the Vietnam War. If we could determine what would have happened in the economy in the absence of the war, then it would be a straightforward matter to compare this historical record with what actually happened and impute the difference. The trick is to determine what would have happened to an economic system that is constantly changing and recording reactions to events as they occur. How does one isolate the effects of one change in this world? How is it possible to distinguish between what would have happened anyway by virtue of the economy operating in its usual way, from what happened as a result of actions taken, deliberately or not, that disturbed the economic system? Any attempt to do so would require a large econometric model that could capture the workings of the economy so as to be able to reconstruct history and be designed to answer the "what if" questions by making suitable assumptions about how various segments of the model would have behaved if some event had not occurred. This methodology has been criticized for its simplistic assumptions of how a complicated economy actually operates, but despite the problems acknowledged by everyone, the simulation technique remains the only way to ask the intriguing questions of what would have happened if . . . , or what was the actual effect of this policy or that.

For example, if one wanted to know the effects of a tax cut, one could just assume that the tax cut was never passed, make some assumptions about the path of other variables in the system, and then compare this economic world with the actual one; the difference between the two worlds would then be attributed to the effects of the tax cut. As imprecise and problematic as this exercise might be, at least some estimates could be ventured over a short-run period. But what of a longer-run period when reactions and responses to the initial change can be made that affect other changes in an endless chain? We are examining the economic effects of a war that was spread out over years, and the reactions to it were uncertain at first, mixed later, and confused throughout.

All this is by way of warning about the interpretation of results of such simulation studies and is an introduction to one such attempt. Economists at the Wharton School, quite aware of the problems involved, made an attempt to examine the economic effects of the Vietnam War, at least for the early years of 1966–69. In this section, some of their results are presented.[14]

The appropriate variables to be controlled in the case of the economic impact of the Vietnam War are defense related ones. Accordingly, defense purchases, military manpower and compensation, and orders for defense capital goods become the items to be adjusted. In addition, nondefense expenditures and tax policy must be considered as well.

Of the initial four scenario options, two were selected as the most important representing the outer boundaries.

OMB

1. The first case simply eliminated all costs directly attributable to the war and assumed that no other expenditures would have been altered. The costs (full) of the war were taken from the Office of Budget and Management (OMB), and hence this case was labeled the OMB approach.

2. Military manpower was assumed constant at 2.7 million.

3. New orders for defense goods were held constant at $16 billion.

In this restrictive case, *none* of the Vietnam expenditures would have been replaced by expenditures in other areas or sectors; simply, no wartime expenditures would have been made with everything else equal.

WEFA

1. The Wharton Economic Forecasting Associates (WEFA) case assumes that defense purchases would have grown at an annual rate of 1.5 percent, the average annual rate for the period 1956–62.
2. Military manpower was held constant at 2.7 million.
3. New orders for defense capital goods were assumed to rise at an annual rate of 4.5 percent.
4. The tax surcharge of 1968 was eliminated.
5. Nondefense expenditures were assumed to grow at an annual rate of 6 percent.

This case (WEFA) permits "normal" growth of nondefense expenditures and permits a tax policy consistent with the assumption that no war took place.

Some of the results of the simulations studies are shown in Table 3.4. The OMB (no war, everything else equal) and the WEFA (no war with adjustments made to defense and nondefense spending and taxes) are shown juxtaposed for easy reference.

Looking first at aggregate demand, the impact of the war was much greater using the OMB assumptions. In 1966, the OMB methodology estimated that GNP in 1972 doll rs was nearly $25 billion higher as a result of the war, and that amount in reases to nearly $50 billion in each of the years from 1967–69. Note th t housing demand and net exports would have been greater and consumption and investment would have been lower had there been no war.

However when one considers a normal trend in government expenditures and the elimination of the tax surcharge, the estimates differ considerably. Looking at the WEFA simulations, the initial impact of the war on the GNP of $10 billion in 1966 rises to about $25 billion in 1967 and 1968, but falls to only $3 billion in 1969. By 1969, then, most of the impact of the war is over, and the GNP is only some $3 billion more than it would have been in the absence of the war. Again without the war, housing and net exports would have been greater. Without the war, purchases from other countries to support the war effort would not have been necessary, and net

Table 3.4
Estimated Impact of No Vietnam War on Selected Economic Series

Item	1966		1967		1968		1969	
	OMB	WEFA	OMB	WEFA	OMB	WEFA	OMB	WEFA
GNP (in bill of 1972$)	-23.7	-9.3	-45.6	-25.5	-58.5	-28.2	-48.7	-3.3
Consumption	-3.5	-1.5	-9.5	-5.2	-15.5	-6.6	-16.1	0.8
Housing expend	0.8	0.1	2.4	1.0	1.5	1.1	1.5	1.1
Investment	-3.0	-0.5	-7.1	-3.1	-10.4	-4.8	-8.4	0.0
Net Exports	1.6	0.5	3.3	1.4	5.7	2.1	6.5	1.7
Unemploy rate (%)	1.1	0.5	2.2	1.3	2.9	1.6	2.7	0.8
Price Indexes (Base = 100)								
GNP deflator	-0.1	0.0	-0.3	-0.2	-0.7	-0.5	-1.6	-1.2
CPI	-0.1	-0.1	-0.3	-0.2	-0.1	-0.8	-2.3	-1.7
WPI	-0.1	-0.1	0.0	0.0	-0.1	-0.1	-0.2	-0.1

Source: Adapted from U.S. Congress, Joint Economic Committee, Wharton Econometric Forecasting Associates, Inc., "A Study in Counter Cyclical Policy," in *Economic Stabilization Policies: The Historical Record, 1962–76;* 95th Congress, 2d Session (Washington D.C.: U.S. Government Printing Office, November 1978), 101, 103, 104.

exports would have expanded. Without the war, more resources would have flowed into the housing sector. In short, by 1969 using the WEFA model, the economy would have returned to its "normal" path, and the impact of the war on the economy would have been minimal.

Of particular interest is the effect of the no war scenario on the labor market. Without the war, many military personnel would have been available for civilian employment. Depending upon the assumptions made regarding the participation in the civilian labor market of these military personnel, the results show up in the unemployment rate. Instead of the tight labor markets found in actuality in this period, the no war scenario leads to unemployment rates that range from nearly 3 percentage points higher than actual experience in the case of the OMB model in 1969 to 1.6 percentage points higher in the WEFA model in the same year. The unemployment data are given in Table 3.4.

The OMB model postulates that lower wages would result in more people leaving the labor market (or not entering it), and hence its unemployment rate remains high. The WEFA model, which attempts to restore normal economic growth paths, results in the unemployment rate falling as more military personnel are absorbed in civilian employment.

Finally, as might be expected, prices would have been lower. Table 3.4 shows that most of the impact on prices occurs in 1969. The CPI and the GNP deflator are between 2–3 percentage points lower than historical levels in the OMB case, and around 1.5 percentage points in the WEFA case. The lower inflation rates in the OMB case reflect the higher unemployment rates in that model, while the WEFA model assumes greater productivity growth that serves to reduce its inflation rate.

These are just some of the results obtained by the Wharton Associates in their simulation studies. In most cases they confirm the trends that might have been anticipated by observation of the historical record. In this sense they are certainly useful as a check on preconceptions.

Yet the world they postulate is forced to be somewhat artificial. This controlled and constrained world limits their ability to obtain more precise magnitudes, but more important, limits their ability to incorporate reactions and responses of economic agents to changing economic conditions. To change one important fact, i.e., that no war took place, and then assume everything else remains the same is clearly not realistic; in the other case, to assume a no war situation and then postulate that historical changes of other variables continue may be more realistic, but not much more so.

In fact one of the major themes of this book is that the war disrupted so many past relationships, and disrupted so much of our economic behavior, that the economy underwent significant changes. So merely extrapolating past economic relations would tend to distort the impact of the war on the society. Instead the war fostered new economic behavior, forced structural changes on the economy, and helped promulgate new institutions.

If people observe their world changing, as an event such as a war would clearly accomplish, then they will likely respond to those changes, again fostering new and different responses, etc. In the end the new world may differ significantly from the old, an eventuality that simulation techniques simply cannot handle.

So without pausing to examine critically the actual results of the simulations, we turn to some of the structural changes that surfaced in this period; changes that argue against the use of simulation models that are forced to create an artificial world against which to measure the real one.

NOTES

1. Doris Kearns, *Lyndon Johnson and the American Dream* (New York: Harper and Row, 1976), 335.

2. Ibid., 251–52.

3. Walter W. Heller, *New Dimensions of Political Economy* (New York: W. W. Norton, 1967), 87.

4. See Robert W. Stevens, *Vain Hopes, Grim Realities* (New York: New Viewpoints, 1976), 75.

5. Edwin L. Dale, "The Inflation Goof," *New Republic* (January 4, 1969).

6. Arthur M. Okun, *The Political Economy of Prosperity* (New York: W. W. Norton, 1970), 71. In the next paragraph, Okun makes a point that will occupy us in the next chapter:

> The January 1966 budget marked the first defeat of the new economics by the old politics since Kennedy's decision in August 1962 to delay a tax-cut recommendation. Even more important, the new economics could not pass its crucial test because of the defense upsurge and the political paralysis of tax rates. The new economists had insisted repeatedly to their critics that the policy of fiscal stimulus would be turned off in time and would be amended to head off inflation when the economy did reach full employment. For political—not economic—reasons, the skeptics won the debate.

7. See the Council of Economic Advisors' analysis in their *Economic Report of the President, 1967*, 42–45.

8. See Arthur Okun, *The Political Economy of Prosperity*, 76–78.

9. See Jean Crockett, Irwin Friend, and Henry Shavell, "The Impact of Monetary Stringency on Business Investment," in U.S. Department of Commerce, *Survey of Current Business* 47 (August 1967): 10–27.

10. Okun, *The Political Economy of Prosperity*, 81.

11. Ibid., 83.

12. See Arthur Okun, "The Personal Tax Surcharge and Consumer Demand, 1968–70," in *Brookings Papers* (Washington D.C.: Brookings Institution, 1971), 167–212; and William L. Springer, "Did the 1968 Surcharge Really Work?" *American Economic Review* 65 (September 1975): 644–59; and the subsequent exchange between the two economists in the *American Economic Review* 67 (March 1977): 166–72.

13. Perhaps Okun put it best:

The difficulties of explaining the movements of private demand and responses of public policy during 1968–69 remind us of how much economists have to learn. They also remind us that changes in attitudes in the private economy can at times swamp decisions of public policy. They argue for humility in our discussions of the economic outlook and for flexibility in the making of policy.

Okun, *Political Economy of Prosperity*, 96.

14. See U.S. Congress, Joint Economic Committee, Wharton Econometric Forecasting Associates, "A Study in Counter Cyclical Policy," in *Economic Stabilization Policies: The Historical Record, 1962–76*, 95th Congress, 2d Session (Washington, D.C.: U.S. Government Printing Office, November 1978).

4 THE CHANGING ECONOMIC STRUCTURE, 1966

The ultimate economic consequences of the Vietnam War can never be known with any degree of precision. The war affected the entire society in so many ways that everyone's life was touched at some point if only by the atmosphere it created. For some, the war presented an opportunity for private gain regardless of questions of morality or justification; no qualms intruded upon their decisions, and no nagging doubts restrained their actions. Many others rejected the war and opposed U.S. involvement in the internal affairs of other nations. For these people, the war was immoral, and anyone who contributed to it, participated in it, or fostered it was subject to condemnation. Of course, there were all shades of opinion between these extremes.

Allowing for the spectrum of views, however, is merely to acknowledge the controversy surrounding all facets of the U.S. involvement in Southeast Asia. It does not reveal which actions were taken because of the war, which were postponed, and which were cancelled; there are no records of which firms adjusted their operations to profit from the war or which ones refused to do so. Similarly we cannot know how many individuals pursued careers they would normally not have, e.g., idealists who escaped the draft in college classrooms and then became educators, or at the other extreme, drafted men who went on to make the military a career.

Clearly the war affected many decisions, but short of a national survey, they cannot be tabulated or measured in some convenient giant matrix. Wars in general have a habit of severely disrupting a society and affecting the decisions of everyone. Many choices have to be made under conditions not conducive to making them: what occupation to pursue; where to live; when to marry, have children, divorce, buy a house, and so on.

Yet the Vietnam War was different in that it was not a total war and thus did not affect the lives of everyone in equal measure. Many were simply bystanders while others made heavy sacrifices. The distribution of the burden was not equally shared. For example, most benefited by the booming economy and made no sacrifices in their living standards. True, taxes did rise somewhat, but they could be paid for out of rising and inflated incomes. There was no need to make any sacrifices in the consumption of durable goods or particular services as was the case in World War II. A large proportion of the sacrifices that were made were confined to the poor who saw their social programs being cut and their expectations for improved lives dashed. The poor sent their sons to the war while the middle and upper classes sent theirs to college to escape the draft. Only when the college deferment was dropped in favor of a lottery, and the draft became more democratic did the more favored groups in the society find fault with the war. As long as it meant just paying for it, the war seemed remote from their daily lives. When the lives of their sons were disrupted, and even threatened, then the war became a reality.

There is no need to belabor the point: many decisions and actions were affected as a result of the war. That we cannot know what these decisions were or how they affected the society and the economy calls for humility in any attempt to account for the consequences of the Vietnam War. All that we can measure in economics are the results of these decisions as they were reflected and registered in conventional measures like inflation, employment, and GNP.

However in addition to these conventional measures, it might be useful to suggest some of the structural changes made in the economy immediately following the Vietnam War escalation. Some of these changes occurred around the year 1966 and can be traced directly to the war; other changes occurred as a result of forces percolating over the years that seemed to come to a head in that year. Still other changes may be unrelated to the war but were heavily influenced by the economy that resulted from the war. Again no magic matrix exists to identify which type of change occurred as a result of the war and which would have happened anyway. All that can be done is to catalog the changes and suggest the category to which they can be attributed. [1]

INFLATION

After a long period of price stability, inflation revived in 1965. In the period 1960–64 for instance, the CPI rose by 1.2 percent and in 1965 by

1.9 percent; in the same periods the WPI rose from zero change to 3.3 percent, and the GNP index rose from 1.3 percent to 2.7 percent. The sharp increase in the CPI occurred in the second quarter of 1965 when the rate jumped from 0.8 percent at annual rates to 2.9 percent. Even a cursory examination at the defense obligations series (see Table 2.1) reveals the Vietnam War as the culprit for the resurrection of inflation. National defense obligations also rose sharply in the same quarter by about eight percent or by 33 percent at an annual rate. While this concurrence seems extraordinary, there is widespread agreement that the inflation of the next decade began here and was a direct result of increased military spending. Table 4.1 provides the necessary data to support that conclusion.

There seems to be no question as to the origin of the inflation, but how much of the subsequent inflation can be accredited to the Vietnam War? Some insight can be gained by looking at the price indexes and defense expenditures on Vietnam. Here the data show the Vietnam buildup occurred in 1965 at the same time that prices began to accelerate. Vietnam spending exploded in 1966 and then the increases tapered off until they began to fall in 1970.

Thus looking only at expenditures in Vietnam, the major contribution to inflation would have been in the years 1966–68; thereafter, as the war wound down, direct spending on Vietnam would not appear to have been responsible for the observed continued price increases.

Table 4.1
Inflation in the Vietnam War Period (Percent Change)

Year	Consumer Price Index (unadj.)	Wholesale Price Index (Unadj.)	GNP Index	National Defense Oblig- ations	Actual Expend Vietnam War
1960–1964	1.2	0.0	1.3	–	–
1965	1.9	3.3	2.7	4.8	16.8
1966	3.4	2.2	3.6	26.8	5700.0
1967	3.0	1.6	2.6	3.2	217.2
1968	4.7	3.1	5.0	7.0	31.8
1969	6.1	4.8	5.6	0.6	8.7
1970	5.5	2.2	5.5	-4.1	-20.1

Source: Price changes calculated from *Economic Report of the President, 1987*; National defense obligations calculated from U.S. Treasury Department, *Bulletins*, various years. For Vietnam expenditures, see Tables 1.1 and 3.2.

Looking at defense obligations data for a better series to measure the economic impact again reveals the enormous buildup in 1966 with the tapering off of obligations coming earlier and falling more rapidly than actual expenditures on Vietnam. Of course, these data refer to total defense obligations and not just to Vietnam alone, and thus it is not as easy to make general statements without further investigation.

Evidently then, *demand pull* inflation was instigated by the Vietnam War expenditures starting in 1965 and continuing in 1966. The gap between actual and potential GNP had been closed by the end of 1965 and further expenditures not fully offset by tax increases clearly resulted in a period of excess demand. With a virtual zero gap between potential and actual GNP, the increase in defense obligations of $16 billion from 1965 to 1966 can serve as an approximation of the amount of excess demand in the economy. The rise in prices was inevitable.[2]

Yet the rise in prices was gradual and slow to develop. Even with the added demand pressures, the legacy of prior price stability meant that inflation was not anticipated or expected to continue in the early part of the period and thus was not built into plans; even by 1968 the rate of change in the CPI was just 4.7 percent and 5 percent in the GNP index. What this implies is that there was time to combat inflation in the early stages if the proper mix of monetary and fiscal policy had been employed. However the expansionary fiscal policy in 1965 combined with a contractionary monetary policy in 1966 created only uncertainty and fears that further government actions would be necessary in the coming years.

The monetary policy that brought about the credit crunch of 1966 was intended to fight the excess demand problem, and as we have seen, the result was a mini recession in 1967. Price increases moderated in 1967 but continued their upward march once the monetary authorities retreated in the face of the financial crisis they created. As defense spending decreased, and the Vietnam War deescalated, can the rise in prices beyond 1967 be attributed to the Vietnam War or to defense spending in general?[3]

Part of that answer can be found in the WEFA study cited in Chapter 3. Using the GNP price deflator as the measure of price changes, the results of that study found that there were small differences between actual history and either model in the early years, 1966–67. In 1968 and 1969 the models begin to diverge from the actual data. Without the war by 1969, inflation would have been lower by one full percentage point using the OMB model (no war, everything else equal) and 0.6 percentage points less using the WEFA model (no war, other variables return to normal paths).

Clearly the war can be blamed for some inflation beyond 1967 according to these results. One study, using different techniques and data, found just the opposite but the conclusions rest on a peculiar definition of demand pressures, and did not allow for expectations (or cost push inflation) to influence the analysis.

But the situation heading into 1968 was different from that at the outset of the war. By 1968 inflation was no longer a possibility, it was a reality and becoming obvious to most people. Since inflation was expected to continue, people began to build it into their price quotations, wage demands, interest rate charges, and so on. Everyone tried to stay ahead of inflation by protecting his own reward; of course, not everyone succeeded at this game, and in the end, most prices tended to rise. What started out as demand inflation was transformed into supply or cost push inflation whereby those who had market power began to demand higher prices or higher wages, even when the demand was not excessive for their output or service.

Cost push inflation is difficult to prove and remains controversial especially to those who deny market power as an explanation for inflation. Those who do favor the concept of cost push or sellers' inflation would find that the economic conditions in 1968 would support their contention: Labor markets were tight with unemployment averaging about 3.6 percent; the growth in labor productivity was leveling off while compensation per hour was rising meaning rising labor costs; manufacturers' usage of capacity was beginning to fall; corporate profits were increasing, and so on. Thus the right set of conditions were present to support the view that cost push inflation had begun to take over from excess demand inflation due to the inability or unwillingness to combat inflation when it first began to threaten. Much has been written about these factors and we will return to some of them in later discussions, but the point is that excess demand may initiate a period of inflation but the effects on the economy do not stop once the source of the excess demand has stopped. Unless fought at the outset, inflation will begin to permeate the economic system and become embodied into all contracts as it winds its way through the system, and as always, those who are able to protect themselves will take actions designed to do so while those who are less powerful will fall behind.

One theory that accounts for these shifts in inflation and attempts to explain the elements of inflation is the theory of core inflation.[4] Less controversial than pure cost push inflation, core inflation still attempts to account for inflation from the cost side as well as the demand side. In the words of Otto Eckstein:

Core inflation [is] defined as the trend rate of increase of the price of aggregate supply. All supply can be traced back to labor and capital, the two primary factors of production. Labor costs are determined by the rate of wage increase adjusted for the productivity trend. Capital costs are set by interest rates, equity prices and the relative price of capital goods. While there are numerous short-lived inflationary elements in the economy, the underlying thrust comes from the gradual rise in the price of labor and capital, the core inflation rate.

The temporary inflation forces are classified into two headings: "shock inflation," such as increases in oil and food prices, and "demand inflation," the classic pull of tight labor and product markets on the price level. Total inflation is the sum of all three sources: core, shock and demand.[5]

According to this theory, core inflation was virtually eliminated in 1965 but began to reappear thereafter as a result of military expenditures as it accounted for 0.9 percent of the inflation rate in 1966, 1.6 percent in 1967, 1.9 percent in 1968, 3.0 percent in 1969 and 4.1 percent in 1970. (See Table 4.2.)

Note how price expectations became increasingly important as an explanatory factor in the inflation rate, along with the phenomenal increase in the cost of capital and the less spectacular increases in wage gains. Also important is the increase in interest rates as tight money in 1966 became embodied into the rate structure. Shock inflation is less important in this period; price shocks, from food and energy sources, would appear in the 1970s.

Of course demand inflation clearly shows up as the main factor in inflation in 1966 and 1967, but note how excess demand becomes less important after 1968 as a source of inflation. The initial price increases due to excess demand were by 1968 incorporated into the long-term expectations of households and firms. Once the short-term inflationary factors have been transferred into long-term expectations, i.e., core inflation, they are likely to persist, and therefore are difficult to combat by ordinary fiscal and monetary policies.

INFLATIONARY EXPECTATIONS

Thus one of the first economic consequences of the Vietnam War and the military buildup was inflation. Not only inflation in the years in which the military spending was initiated and piled on top of a smoothly function-

Table 4.2
Core, Shock, and Demand Inflation, 1965–70 (Percent Change)

	1965	1966	1967	1968	1969	1970
Unit Labor Cost Trend (weight .65)	0.9	1.0	1.3	1.7	2.6	3.3
"Equilibrium" Wage Gains.................	3.9	4.0	4.4	4.6	5.2	5.6
Actual Wage Gains	3.4	4.4	4.9	6.2	6.7	6.7
Price Expectations......................	1.5	1.7	2.0	2.4	2.9	3.4
Unemployment Rate (level)	4.5	3.8	3.8	3.6	3.5	5.0
Productivity Trend	2.9	3.1	3.0	2.9	2.5	2.2
Actual Productivity Gains	3.4	2.5	1.6	3.2	-0.2	0.1
+ Capital Cost Trend (weight .35)	0.0	0.9	2.1	2.2	3.7	5.6
Actual Rental Price of Capital	2.2	6.4	0.1	6.8	11.1	5.6
Aftertax Cost of Capital..................	5.3	3.8	-6.3	1.7	-1.3	-3.7
Prime Rate (level)	4.54	5.63	5.63	6.28	7.95	7.91
New High-Grade Corp. Bond Rate (level)..	4.54	5.44	5.77	6.48	7.68	8.50
Price Expectations......................	1.5	1.8	2.2	2.7	3.3	3.9
Dividend-Price Ratio—S&P 500 (level)	3.0	3.3	3.2	3.1	3.2	3.8
= Core Inflation Rate	0.6	0.9	1.6	1.9	3.0	4.1
Shock Inflation Rate.......................	0.3	0.7	0.0	0.2	0.5	0.4
WPI—Farm Products.....................	4.4	7.3	-5.6	2.5	6.4	1.7
WPI—Fuels	1.8	2.5	2.3	-1.1	2.0	5.3
Trade-Weighted Exchange Rate	0.0	0.0	-0.1	-1.3	-0.1	-2.5
Social Security Tax Rate (difference)........	-0.002	0.014	0.003	0.001	0.004	0.000
Minimum Wage ($/hour).................	1.250	1.250	1.387	1.583	1.600	1.600
Demand Inflation Rate.....................	0.7	1.4	1.2	2.1	2.0	1.4
Capacity Utilization in Manufacturing (level)	0.895	0.911	0.869	0.870	0.862	0.794
Unemployment Rate (level)	4.5	3.8	3.8	3.6	3.5	5.0
Consumer Price Index	1.6	3.0	2.8	4.2	5.4	5.9

Source: Otto Eckstein, *Tax Policy and Core Inflation*, for the Joint Economic Committee, 96th
Congress, 2d Session (Washington, D.C.: U.S. Government Printing Office, April 10, 1980),
28.

ing economy, but in subsequent years as well. Failure to combat it in the
early stages meant that inflationary expectations were allowed to develop
and influence the core rate of inflation, i.e., price increases became built-in.
This is the second economic consequence of the Vietnam War. Whereas
inflation was virtually nonexistent prior to 1965, it became increasingly
important as the war continued. According to the Gallup polls, 76 percent
of the people polled expected prices to rise in the coming year in 1965; in
1966 81 percent expected prices to go up in the next six months; and by
1967, even as price increases moderated, 46 percent of those polled
favored a wage freeze for the duration of the Vietnam War.

As inflationary expectations develop, people spend more time and effort trying to stay ahead of inflation by arranging their affairs to avoid being hurt by rising prices. Everyone tries to minimize his or her cash holdings, households begin switching funds from savings to checking accounts only when necessary, corporate treasurers are busy shifting funds between short-term assets, and banks start demanding a premium for loans, and so on. These actions require the preoccupation of firms and households with economic matters. The cost of activity designed to avert economic losses caused by inflation are many as attention is diverted from productive activity to the mere rearrangement of portfolios. The cost is referred to as a "dead weight loss" by economists because it involves unproductive activity.[6] As inflation continued for more than a decade later, these inflationary expectations continued as well and became even worse in the 1970s. Over the years the sources of inflation changed, of course, but there was no doubt that inflation became commonplace.

Still later, as a result of a decade of inflation, there developed a reluctance to utilize whatever fiscal and monetary policy was necessary to revive a sluggish economy because of fears of reviving inflation. This is not to attribute the failure to employ macroeconomic policies to the Vietnam War but only to indicate one of the consequences of the failure to address price increases before they became part of the core inflation, and that occurred in the year under scrutiny, 1966.

THE GUIDEPOST PROGRAM

The program of voluntary wage and price controls, called the guideposts by the Kennedy administration that initiated them in 1962, was another, related casualty that occurred in 1966. It can be argued that the program would have collapsed anyway at some time, and that is certainly a plausible deduction. Yet it did occur in 1966 when the program became obsolete by conditions caused essentially by the military expenditures on Vietnam.

Recall that the guidepost program was designed to combat inflation by proposing that wages should rise according to the average increase in productivity experienced by the entire economy. That is if the average increase in labor productivity in a period were 3.2 percent, wages could rise by 3.2 percent. Labor costs would not increase, hence there would be no pressure to raise prices or profit margins. The productivity gains would be shared equally by all. An argument can be made here that supports the view that the guideposts would have collapsed anyway. Why would organized labor favor a policy that kept labor's share of the output constant when labor's productivity was increasing? Many labor leaders and firms were opposed to the whole idea from the start, of course, and many more could have been expected to join them in time.

Again, however, this was an educational program designed to teach both workers and firms of the benefits to the *nation* of limiting their demands to what productivity warrants. The Council of Economic Advisors stressed that the guideposts were just guides, and there were many exceptions and allowances to the general rules. The guidepost policy was voluntary and lacked sanctions but did manage to avoid the bureaucracy of more formal types of incomes policies.

Whether they restrained wages and prices according to the formula is debatable, but at least one researcher found that the program did work to some extent. After examining the evidence, John Sheahan concluded, "They add up to a convincing case that wage behavior in manufacturing became more restrained in the four years following presentation of the guideposts than it had been in the preceding decade."[7] The numerical estimates of just how effective appear rather modest, from 0.8 percent to 1.6 percent for combined wage and price restraint in the period 1962–65. However the results must be considered in light of the general price stability over the period.

In 1966 this initial attempt of government to intervene in the wage and price decisions, albeit on a voluntary basis, began to unravel. Once food, housing, and other services prices rose, by 5 percent, 2.4 percent and about 2.6 percent, respectively, from 1965 to 1966, and the rate of growth of productivity began to diminish, asking workers to adhere to the guideposts would have meant asking them to accept a decline in their real wages. Organized labor joined with firms to declare the guideposts unworkable and obsolete. The end really came in midsummer of 1966 when the airline machinists strike was settled by wage and fringe benefit increases of over 5 percent, far in excess of the guideposts. Other collective bargaining agreements in other industries indicated that the wage increases granted in 1966 were substantially higher than in the period 1961–65 with increases in 1966 averaging 4.4 percent where they had been 3.2 percent in 1964 and 3.8 percent in 1965.[8]

Gradually the guideposts were ignored as violations of their provisions became routine. The administration continued to jawbone for wage and price restraint but to no avail.[9] The guideposts simply faded away—another casualty of inflation and the Vietnam War.

THE WAR ON POVERTY

The War on Poverty was initiated in the Kennedy administration at the urging of the Council of Economic Advisors (CEA) led by Walter Heller. Robert Lampman, a staff economist, had studied the problem and convinced Heller and through him, the president, that the New Frontier had failed to address this national problem. President Kennedy instructed the CEA to study the problem further and develop programs to combat poverty, presumably in time to make it a campaign issue in 1964.[10] The political wisdom of making poverty a campaign issue did not have to be faced, however, and the whole question was passed on to the Johnson administration.

When asked if the CEA should continue its work on poverty analysis and program development, Johnson, the populist, declared, "I'm interested. I'm sympathetic. Go ahead. Give it the highest priority. Push ahead full tilt." In his first State of the Union address he proclaimed, "This administration today, here and now, declares unconditional war on poverty in America."

The funds allocated for the task never did match the rhetoric, but The Equal Opportunity Act that was passed in August of 1964 did recognize the changing character of poverty and did incorporate new approaches to its elimination. The Act provided for a series of programs, some experimental and others traditional, targeted at specific groups of disadvantaged with the goal of lifting people out of poverty by providing them the means and the motivation to seek self-improvement. In effect the federal government bypassed the state and local governments to reach directly to certain agencies and communities to administer the programs directly. These community action programs included Head Start, VISTA, Job Corps, Neighborhood Youth Corps, Family Planning, Legal Assistance, College Work-Study, and many others.

Evaluating the success of these short-run programs has proved extremely difficult, and whether a longer-term commitment to them would have provided the necessary information to make a judgment must be left to others to decide.[11] The point here is that such a long-term commitment to the elimination of poverty did not exist, and the first signs of retreat occurred in 1966. One look at Table 4.3 is sufficient to show the difficulty of funding the war on poverty while conducting the war in Vietnam, and the data illustrate the case that butter was sacrificed for guns.

The war on poverty was fought with insufficient funds, and this lack of resources was evident right from the beginning. Less than a billion dollars was allocated in 1965 to the Office of Economic Opportunity (OEO), the

Table 4.3
Office of Economic Opportunity Budgets, 1965–68 (in Millions of Dollars)

Fiscal Year	Budget Request	Authorization	Appropriation
1965	$ 947.5	$ 947.5	$ 800.0*
1966	1500.0	1785.0	1500.0
1967	1750.0	1750.0	1687.5
1968	2060.0	1980.0	1773.0

* Appropriation for less than a full year.

Source: Sar A. Levitan, *The Great Society's Poor Law: A New Approach to Poverty* (Baltimore: Johns Hopkins Press, 1969), 93.

agency set up in the White House to administer the programs. The opportunity to secure more funds and expand the antipoverty programs from a liberal and receptive Congress was gradually lost as President Johnson surrendered the initiative.

It is evident that the administration did not pursue the poverty program vigorously for it cut the budget request of OEO for the fiscal year 1966 from $3.4 billion to $1.75 billion. Thus even before Congress forced the president to cut domestic spending in order to secure funding for the Vietnam War, the administration was willing to cut antipoverty spending on its own. In short, the administration began to decrease its commitment to fighting poverty in 1966. Johnson apparently did worry about losing his "passport to historical immortality." As he declared later, "Losing the Great Society was a terrible thought, but not so terrible as the thought of being responsible for America's losing a war to the Communists. Nothing could possibly be worse than that."[12]

In the following year, OEO reduced its request for funds by nearly a billion dollars in a movement of self-inflicted restraint. Congress also helped to restrain OEO as it voted more and more varied programs without increasing the funds necessary to carry them out. Thus the funds had to be spread over more and more programs, robbing them of their effectiveness. These actions of the administration and Congress continued until the early 1970s when the entire antipoverty program was slowly dismantled. With the dismantling went the entire community action approach to fighting poverty, which the Equal Opportunity Act had incorporated. The experimentation appeared to be over, and a reversion to more traditional approaches would soon follow.

In summary, the antipoverty program that was initiated with such fanfare became an early casualty of the Vietnam War. Even before it was necessary for budgetary reasons, the Johnson administration became preoccupied with the Vietnam War and neglected the other war. In reducing its request for funds for fiscal year 1966, the administration signaled its readiness to retreat even before the enemy, poverty, was encountered. True the whole exercise called attention to the problem of poverty amidst affluence, and other programs, such as Medicare, were developed as a result, but it still remains that more could easily have been accomplished were it not the case that Johnson became obsessed with the situation in Southeast Asia. In the end the real casualty was the commitment to do anything to fight poverty in the United States; it would later become possible to assert that we had tried to fight poverty through direct government action, and the fight was lost. In this view it follows that the federal government should refrain from attempting to alleviate poverty and recognize the Biblical admonition that the poor will always be with us.

REVOLUTION OF RISING EXPECTATIONS

The mid-1960s also witnessed the explosion of the black ghettos. Riots broke out in Watts, Newark, Chicago, Detroit, and many other cities. They began in 1965 and increased dramatically in 1966 and 1967. The causes of these riots were many and varied, but according to the Kerner Commission appointed to investigate them, many of the causes were economic in character—inferior housing, education, unemployment, and lack of health care and sanitary conditions. Indeed the Kerner Commission concluded that "Our nation is moving toward two basic societies, one black, one white—separate and unequal."[13] White racism was the cause.

The civil rights movement for political power, for access to public facilities, and for an end to racial discrimination in every area, had begun in earnest in the early 1960s and had raised the expectations of blacks that years of discrimination could be reversed. Now the disillusionment with the slow progress being made in many areas was coming to the surface.

Under these conditions, the Equal Opportunity Act, with its emphasis on community involvement in identifying and solving problems, would appear to be tailor-made to address the problems of the black community. It did not work out that way. The OEO found itself in the middle of the black militants and the white backlash. The black militants found that the programs did not go far enough and stopped cooperating with the OEO, while the white power structure feared and resisted black involvement and advancement. Many black groups continued to work with the OEO, of course, and the OEO itself recognized the problems and tried to work around them.

The civil rights activists, however, became openly hostile to the OEO and withdrew their support. Programs that became too critical of whites, such as the antiwhite plays of LeRoi Jones (who has since changed his name to Imamu Amiri Baraka), caused great consternation in the white community; and programs to increase the literacy and political awareness of poor blacks were not funded at all due to political pressure from white groups.[14] In the meantime, blacks *felt* that they were disproportionally represented on the battlefields of Vietnam since they were being drafted at a higher rate than whites, many of whom were in college classrooms. The actual count of Vietnam veterans does not support the contention that blacks were disproportionally represented in the war; the data suggest that they were proportionally represented at approximately 10 percent. Nevertheless the perception of overrepresentation was evident and frequently voiced, and in the end, facts cannot compete with emotional responses. So in this case, perceptions were important because they could and did influence behavior.

It would be naive to suggest that these events were not connected by black leaders, especially so when the funds for the war on poverty quickly began to decline after the fanfare in 1965. Whatever expectations were raised by the "war" on poverty were soon dashed by the war 10,000 miles away. Consider the reflections of Martin Luther King:

A few years ago there was a shining moment in that struggle. It seemed as if there was a real promise of hope for the poor—both black and white—through the Poverty Program. There were experiments, hopes, new beginnings. Then came the build-up in Vietnam and I watched the program broken and eviscerated as if it were some idle political plaything of a society gone mad on war, and I knew that America would never invest the necessary funds or energies in rehabilitation of its poor so long as adventures like Vietnam continued to draw men and skills and money like some demonic destructive suction tube. So I was increasingly compelled to see the war as an enemy of the poor and to attack it as such.[15]

The betrayal of these expectations could have entered into the equation that justified the rioting in 1966 and 1967. It would be equally naive to suggest that the cause of the riots was the decline in funding of OEO. Years of discrimination were sufficient to explain the uprisings in the ghettos, and many local concerns were germane to particular instances.

Yet the betrayal of rising expectations, some of which may have been created by the war on poverty, cannot be dismissed as a possible cause of the inchoate revolution in the black communities.[16] To some unspecified extent the war in Vietnam and the decline in commitment to the improvement of the nation's poor, so many of them black, must be included as a cause of the social unrest in the ghettos. That these events converged in the turning- point year of 1966 may well be coincidental, but it is inserted here as a reminder of the many ramifications of military adventures at the expense of domestic matters.

THE SLOWDOWN IN PRODUCTIVITY GROWTH

One of the fascinating and puzzling developments that occurred in the mid-1960s was the decline in productivity growth. Up to the present, no satisfactory explanation has been provided for the observed fall in the rate of growth of this significant magnitude for the U.S. economy.[17] In fact too many explanations have been offered, which invariably is an indication of confusion rather than enlightenment. The range of determinants runs from too much government regulation or tax provisions affecting capital investment and lack of expenditures on research and development, to the change in workers' attitudes toward work, and the shift from manufacturing to service industries. That no one variable or even groups of variables can account for the decline is evidence that the explanation is a complex one.

Of course, the measurement of productivity is a difficult task, the more so the more aggregate the data. Everyone admits the problems of measurement, but the data, however measured, do support the claim that something happened to the growth of productivity in the U.S. economy.[18]

It is not the purpose of this section to enter into the debate nor to provide a complete list of the possible explanatory factors. The data in Table 4.4 are supplied as evidence that something happened to productivity, but no claim for accuracy is implied and no detailed explanations are attempted.

There are many ways to measure productivity, and the means shown in Table 4.4 is just one of them; however, any measurement of productivity would reveal the same trends if not the same numbers. The decline in productivity growth actually started in 1965 when the rate of growth of nonfarm business output per hour fell from 3.9 percent to 2.5 percent and then to 2.1 percent in 1966. However the rate of growth of productivity, being procyclical, picked up again in 1967 and then fell precipitously in 1973 and 1974 (when it became negative by 2.2 percent). These dates also identify the business cycle in the United States. When output increases in

Table 4.4
Productivity in the Business Sector, 1947–85 (Average Annual Percent Change)

Period	Output per Hour of All Persons	
	Business Sector	Nonfarm Business Sector
1947–1965	3.3	2.7
1966–1972	2.0	1.7
1973–1979	0.6	0.5
1980–1983	1.2	1.2
1983–1988P	1.7	1.4

p = preliminary

Source: Calculated from data in the *Economic Report of the President, 1989*.

the upswing, productivity growth tends to increase as well since labor is relatively fixed; when output falls, as in 1973–74, productivity growth tends to fall as well since labor is retained for some time before layoffs occur. Hence the growth of productivity varies directly with the business cycle. From 1973 onward the rate of growth of productivity has remained below historical standards and even in the recovery years of the late 1980s, the rates of growth were below those of the early 1960s. Clearly productivity growth has fallen relative to the past record and that decline started in earnest in the mid-1960s.

Again the mid-1960s stand out as a period when the economy changed in a fundamental way—in this case in an essentially unexplained decline in the rate of growth of productivity. It is an important measure since productivity is perhaps the most important indicator of a nation's ability to provide a rising standard of living for its residents and in the 1990s, an indicator of its ability to compete in the international market. For the standard of living to rise, people must produce more and more with their resources, otherwise the division of less goods among more people must result in a decline. Beginning in the 1980s, when the United States became a debtor nation, the situation became even worse since to repay the debt, some of national output had to be paid to foreigners which means less is left over for domestic residents. If productivity is falling, there will be even less left over, and hence a slower increase in the standard of living is inevitable.

There is no question of the importance of productivity but there is a question of how much, if any, can be attributed to the Vietnam War. Here the answers are far less reliable and problematic. It might be argued, for instance, that the best brains were enticed by the military establishment and hence innovations in the productive process or in the introduction of new goods were foregone in favor of superior military weaponry; or it might be argued that most of the R & D funds were garnered by the military with similar results. Perhaps inflation and high interest rates discouraged capital investment, or tight labor markets encouraged sloth. It is doubtful if any of these or other variables can be directly linked to the Vietnam War, and thus the war as a causal factor in the decline in productivity must remain tenuous and speculative. All that can be said with any degree of certainty is that something happened around the time the Vietnam War escalated, but whether that was coincidental or not is unresolved; all that is necessary here is to establish that somewhere about 1966 the economy experienced a severe blow to one of its most significant ingredients, and that blow represented a sharp break with the past in that productivity behaved erratically and failed to recover even as the economy boomed. In the 1970s another sharp break occurred around 1973, but whether the two breaks are related or due to the same set of factors remains to be established. The situation in 1973 is further complicated by the emerging energy problems that compound the difficulties of explaining the drop in productivity.

DECLINE OF LIBERALISM AND FISCAL POLICY

The financing of the Vietnam War delivered a major blow to liberalism and accelerated the drift toward conservatism. Keynesian countercyclical fiscal policy, barely becoming acceptable, and liberalism, barely recrudescent, were early casualties of the war. Indeed it is almost possible to assign a date to the decline of liberalism and the fiscal policy that was identified with it.

Again the year 1966 registered the disillusionment with fiscal policy and the inability of the federal government to manage the economy with the failure to enact a tax increase. The economic consequences of that failure have already been outlined, but it is important to reiterate that the administration was well aware of the need for a tax increase but allowed political factors to overrule economic imperatives. As a result, fiscal policy "veered off course," wrote Arthur Okun, adding,

The January 1966 budget marked the first defeat of the new economics by the old politics since Kennedy's decision in August 1962 to delay a tax-cut recommendation. Even more important, the new economics could not pass its crucial test because of the defense upsurge and the political paralysis of tax rates. The new economists had insisted repeatedly to their critics that the policy of fiscal stimulus would be turned off in time and would be amended to head off inflation when the economy did reach full employment. For political—not economic—reasons, the skeptics won the debate.[19]

Walter Heller, writing of this same period noted,

One wistfully concludes that were it not for Vietnam, early 1966 would have found us comfortably contemplating the form and size of the fiscal dividends needed to keep us on the road to full employment, rather than considering what further actions might be needed to ease the strain on our productive capacity and deal with the vexing and perplexing problem of inflation.[20]

Thus in a few short years, the belief and trust in the federal government's ability to manage the economy went from buoyant confidence to cynical skepticism. The new economics became defensive and Keynesian economics soon was put in quotation marks to register an implied disapproval. Critics and some advocates had always maintained that stimulating an economic system was easier than applying the brakes, that managing recessions was easier than managing prosperity.

Now the nature of the bias was exposed and macroeconomic policies were asymmetrical. It did not matter that the fault lay more with politics than economics; it is easy for conservatives to condemn what they had opposed anyway. Yet since some controls over the economy were essential, monetary policy was pushed into the forefront to occupy the vacuum. Favored by conservatives anyway, monetary policy was now elevated by default to the principle means of management.

With its acceptance came also the primary emphasis on securing price stability and maintaining orderly markets, for monetary policy is best suited to minimize price fluctuations that upset asset values. So the problems of portfolio managers were given precedence over other societal problems, many of which lost funding or were forced to seek solutions by other means, or were made to wait for another time.

Clearly the movement toward monetary policy involved much more than the choice of alternative instruments to control the demand side of the economy. More important was the not very subtle shift in philosophy that favored the protection of asset values of higher income classes to the redress of social ills that were directed toward the less fortunate members of the society. As we shall see, this shift away from fiscal policy to monetary policy was to outlast the Vietnam War and was accompanied by the decline in the zeal to correct social problems through government actions.

DESTABILIZING FINANCIAL INNOVATIONS

Aside from the shift toward monetary policy, the credit crunch of 1966 fostered the growth of innovations in the banking and financial sector. These innovations have resulted in a decline in the effectiveness of monetary policy and/or a shift in who is affected by monetary policy. In either case they have made the conduct of monetary policy more complex, more difficult, and in the end more destabilizing.

Whenever there are barriers to the conduct of business as usual, such as slow monetary growth or rigid regulations in the face of dramatic pressures, there is the invitation to circumvent these conditions by innovations.[21] Thus, for instance, monetarism, or control over a monetary aggregate, is likely to be self-defeating; so too are inflexible regulations that become too stringent for the prevailing conditions.

The period under review, 1966–69, was a good example of these tendencies. The slow growth of the money supply—the credit crunch—combined with the interest rate ceiling imposed by Regulation Q, set in motion the attempts to avoid the problems caused by the credit crunch and any repetitions of it thereafter. Several financial innovations were accomplished to foil any attempt by the monetary authorities to restrain the actions of money market participants. Recall that in 1966, interest rates rose above those set by Regulation Q (that set the maximum interest rate that could be paid on time deposits) and funds flowed out of institutions affected (disintermediation) such as the thrifts; with higher mortgage interest rates, the housing industry was crippled. With the demand for funds high and the supply low, banks sought ways to satisfy the demand and satisfy their long-time customers as well.

Unable to avoid Regulation Q as they had in the past by issuing certificates of deposit (CDs) at market interest rates, banks chose to avoid it altogether by forming one-bank holding companies. Banks could now raise funds by issuing commercial paper whose market interest rates escaped the control of the Federal Reserve. This avenue of escape was partially closed later, but the ability of the Federal Reserve to control broader measures of credit conditions, e.g. M2 or M3, was severely tested, and the fragility of the banking system was increased as these bank holding companies increased the debt to equity ratios over that of other sectors of the banking system.

In another development, banks established branches offshore where deposits are regulated by the country of location not the Federal Reserve. Many of these branches were merely small offices or shells for that is all that is needed to avoid the U.S. regulations. Furthermore offshore banks also borrowed Eurodollars to lend to foreign affiliates of U.S. firms and both escaped Federal Reserve control. Of course, large banks in the United States also borrowed Eurodollars that were free of reserve requirements until 1969 and also escaped controls.

In a related development, foreign banks set up additional branches in the United States and began lending to U.S. firms from funds raised in Europe. These deposits were not recorded in U.S. monetary data at the time and thus were not considered in determining monetary policy nor in gauging its success or failure. Clearly large firms and large banks found it relatively easy to escape the stringent monetary policy of the period.

Another means to avoid reserve requirements or interest rate ceilings was found in repurchase agreements and in the federal funds market. In a repurchase agreement, the bank sells a government security to a firm or agency of government for a short period with the promise to buy it back at a stated price that includes interest. The buyer gains in the form of interest on what are essentially demand deposits (not permitted at the time) since the sales proceeds are redeposited in a demand deposit. The bank gains as it has use of the funds over the period. Similar results appear in the federal funds market where banks borrow from each other on an unsecured basis when short-term funds are needed.

Finally in an effort to avoid budgetary deficits and protect selected markets like housing and agriculture from the ravages of high interest rates experienced in 1966, the federal government through various agencies began to intervene in financial markets to increase the flow of funds and reduce interest rates to these favored markets. While the housing and agricultural markets benefit from government intervention and protection, monetary policy was made more difficult since some markets were now shielded from the effects, or the policy had to be pursued with greater severity to have any effect.

What is true of off-budget items is true in general as a result of financial innovations—monetary policy has been either circumvented or made less effective. While not due solely to the economic conditions surrounding 1966 (after all many of these avenues were available prior to that period), much of the impetus for developing them can be traced to the desire to avoid a repetition of the credit conditions in that year.

CHALLENGES TO INSTITUTIONS

The decline in liberalism was helped along by an intransigent president who refused to yield his neo-New Deal dream to the war he essentially elevated to a crusade. When his promise of guns and butter did not materialize the way was open for an alternative vision. If government could not or would not solve problems perhaps it was causing the problems in the first place. Gradually this view, mixed as it was with the identification of Johnson's brand of liberalism with the war, obtained more and more credence and more and more adherents. Critics of an active federal government were always present and now they had some evidence to support their case.

Government was not to be trusted. Even if its goals were laudable, it could not efficiently accomplish them and could even make them unattainable. Better to leave the solving of problems to the private sector. Moreover, take as much of the discretionary powers away from public officials as possible and require that they obey rules. Hence the rise of monetarism, which suggested that monetary influences were the most important in the economy, and control over the money supply should be the sole aim of the authorities. Even here, the best method to achieve monetary control was to require that the money supply grow at a steady rate—a rule. In fiscal policy, the government ought to balance its budget annually—another rule. Rules replaced discretion in this conservative ethic and although never totally accepted, many were heavily influenced by the basic message—distrust in the ability and the efficacy of government to manage the economy.

This distrust of government, again fostered by the deceptions, lies, and misrepresentations of the war, was to linger for the next decade. The Nixon administrations were only to add to the already evident disillusionment with the actions of public officials and with government in general. This attitude is always present with reference to politicians, but was now being extended to cover all governmental attempts at managing its affairs.

Distrust in the military followed in much the same way. The conduct of the war with its wildly inaccurate forecasts of military requirements, with its inept tactics, and, as the war evolved, with its declarations of victories, ludicrously expressed by body counts, and so on, did little to enhance the reputation of the military. Nor did it further the cause of those who favor military solutions as victory eluded the superior forces of a great nation. Eventually a "Vietnam syndrome" emerged in which further adventures and exploits of this kind were prohibited by the experience of the war in Southeast Asia.

Perhaps these challenges would have been mounted in time anyway but were hastened by the atmosphere created by the war. They are, after all, not novel ideas but have been expressed many times in different ways. In this period they may have emanated from and were characterized by frustration, generated by the war.

In a similar vein, there were eruptions in other parts of the society that reverberated on existing institutions, and it seemed to many that the social fabric was being torn apart. One of these was the accord between organized labor and management that ensured a long period of industrial peace. After the end of World War II there was a struggle between labor and management for control over the workplace. Organized labor wanted to protect and extend its gains made in the preceding decade, while management wanted to reverse those gains and return to the relationships that existed prior to the depression. Put simply, the accord reached allowed labor to control the labor side through the right to bargain collectively, to set membership conditions, the collection of dues, and so on; management maintained control over the workplace, and over investment and production decisions.

The accord lasted as long as the parties represented the groups they served. Corporate power did not go unchecked but small businesses were hardly in a position to challenge the dominance of large firms. However organized labor did witness an erosion of its influence. Union membership declined steadily from the end of World War II from approximately 35 percent of the nonagricultural labor force in 1945 to 23 percent in 1966. Over that time period too many jobs were created in the nonunion sector for those who were not tied to the labor union movement. These jobs were in the service sector and were filled by women, minorities, and the young. These groups, long ignored by the labor union movement, now found their voices, and they began to object to the conditions that relegated them to low-paying, dead-end jobs. The feminist movement began to call attention to the job and wage disparities; the civil rights movement forced these and other issues on the nation; and the youth of the nation, faced with these labor market conditions or military service in Vietnam, often chose to escape the country or to escape the dismal prospects by resorting to crime or to drugs.

Meanwhile the tight labor markets, together with the gains made in the form of social reforms—unemployment compensation, social insurance—

permitted labor to feel more independent of past restraints.[22] The freedom found expression in additional strikes, in the willingness to change jobs, or in other challenges to corporate power.

This, in brief, describes the breakdown of the old rules of the game with regard to the proper place of various groups and the proper roles they were supposed to play. From this period on it would be impossible to ignore the demands of those previously excluded from implicit or explicit agreements. The labor movement was fragmented and would begin to sacrifice power in its attempt to stabilize its eroding base. Later the continuing growth of the service sector would exacerbate organized labor's problems. In this period, it is sufficient to note that challenges were being made to both organized labor's traditional role and representation and to the traditional vision of corporate control and power.

One last consequence of the war to be considered was the fragmentation of the labor movement. Organized labor's response to the war was ambiguous, to put it kindly. The leadership AFL-CIO, led by George Meany, supported the war and urged victory, sometimes inferring at any cost. Organized labor was largely missing from the ranks of those opposed to the war, and its absence was noted with much regret. Individual unions, and other union leaders, such as Walter Reuther, did object to the war and voiced concerns over the morality of war-induced prosperity, even if more employment was created as a consequence. Many felt that the prosperity brought no lasting gains to labor anyway.

Perhaps the wounds of the divisions opened up in this period have healed over time, as other concerns have replaced those emanating from a war-torn society, but who is to document the respect lost for organized labor by the youth of the time who sought allies and support from those who had been regarded as traditional sources of dissent?[23]

OTHER DEVELOPMENTS IN OR AROUND 1966

Capacity Utilization

The year 1966 also saw the peak of manufacturers' use of their capacity. Manufacturers were using an increasing amount of their facilities from 1962 to 1965 going from a rate of utilization of 81 percent to 90 percent in 1965. In the peak year of 1966, the rate climbed to over 91 percent but it fell quickly and has never returned to this rate up to 1988, where it stood at nearly 84 percent.

Since 1966, then, the U.S. economy has been saddled with excess capacity, and unemployed capital is just as much an economic loss as unemployed labor. Not all industries experienced the same decline as did total manufacturing, of course, and some industries simply varied capacity usage over the business cycle. Still over the years since 1966 the trend is unmistakable—U.S. firms are using less of their facilities, particularly in the nondurable manufacturing areas.

Whether this development is related to the decline in productivity is not clear but the possibility does exist. It is more likely to be related to the topic of the next section—corporate profits. Neither is it clear that the Vietnam War is a logical explanation for the trend. In either case, the existence of excess capacity is undesirable for any economy and especially for one that is struggling with economic growth. Business firms are unlikely to invest in the latest capital equipment, likely to be more productive, when they already have the capacity to meet demand; when demand is sluggish, as is the case for a stagnating economy, the situation is even more acute. But the failure of investment to grow not only means a stagnating economy on the demand side but a slow growing one on the supply side. Without growth, fewer jobs and opportunities are created, productivity declines, and the standard of living will not increase. The U.S. economy can afford none of these conditions in the 1990s when it must grow to repay its debt in a very competitive world. Indeed the decline in the manufacturing sector is clearly reflected in the decline in capacity usage as the rest of the world has forced many U. S. firms to retrench and idle their equipment.

Corporate Profits

Bowles, Gordon, and Weisskopf wrote of the decline in corporate profits after 1966 in terms of the decline in the corporate sector's ability to control economic agents with whom it deals. They pointed to the decline in the terms of trade, to the increase in financial security and hence independence of workers, and to the increase in the cost of raw materials as responsible for the decline in profits and for the erosion of control and power of corporations in the post-1966 period.[24]

No one would quarrel with the explanation of the decline in corporate profits as a result of the increases in the cost of raw materials—oil for example. Nor would anyone contest the possible fall in profits due to increasing competition from abroad and the decline in the terms of trade.

Profits would be expected to fall under these circumstances, and these remain plausible explanations for the post-1966 trend. The evidence that labor has become more secure and thus more independent of corporate domination is possible but less defensible, and that explanation must be put aside for the time being.

The existence of excess capacity demonstrated in the previous section accounts for much of the cyclical fluctuations in corporate profits. The higher the rate of capacity utilization, the greater is output and hence overhead costs are spread over more units and profits are higher and vice versa. Yet even after removing the effects of excess capacity, Martin Feldstein and Lawrence Summers found that the rate of profit had begun to fall in the 1965–66 period.[25]

The definition and measurement of corporate profits is not as straightforward as would appear. Several questions arise: how to treat interest payments; how to adjust for inventory valuation adjustments and capital gains; how to handle depreciation allowances; and what measurement of capital stock to use are just a few of the difficulties involved. Using different measurements from Feldstein and Summers, William Nordhaus reached different conclusions: "Over the postwar period the share of measured profits has declined in a dramatic way."[26] In the longer run, he expected the share of profit to depend upon policy measures designed to affect the share and the state of the economy.

The issue is a complex one and cannot be discussed fully here. The point is that profits, at least in the corporate nonfinancial sector, declined in the period under review and did not recover within that period. Indeed, Nordhaus began his article with this statement: "By most reckonings corporate profits have taken a dive since 1966."[27] The variety of reasons given for the decline in profits and the various forecasts offered demonstrate again the complexity of the issue but one conclusion stands out: corporate profits declined on or about the year 1966. Without attempting to explain the evidence, or even to present it with all the detail that would be required, we will simply accept the fact and note that it concurs with other evidence that suggest that 1966 was a pivotal year for the U.S. economy.

Before leaving the topic, it might be interesting to see what the simulation models tell us about corporate profits in the early years of the war. Without the war, corporate profits would have been even less; in either model, corporate profits before taxes would have been less than the actual record (or alternatively stated, the war boosted corporate profits). For 1966 through 1969, for example, the OMB model (no war, everything else constant) shows that corporate profits would have been less by $8.4 billion in 1966, $11.3 billion in 1967, $11.3 billion in 1968, and $2.0 billion in 1969. Using the WEFA model (no war, adjustments made to return to normal paths) the data for the same period are $2.6 billion in 1967, $5.5 billion in 1968, and $3.0 billion in 1968, but for 1969, corporate profits would have been larger by $11.5 billion.[28] The Wharton economists noted that this result was accounted for by the labor market conditions caused by the war. The war reduced the unemployment rate, created a tight labor market, and shifted the income shares in favor of wages and away from profits. Without the war, profit shares would have recovered in the WEFA model by 1969 and been greater than the actual record, and nearly so in the OMB model.

SUMMARY AND CONCLUSIONS

The enumeration of developments surrounding the year 1966 clearly reveals that some fundamental changes occurred in the structure of the U.S. economy. These changes were to affect the functioning of the economy for years after the events that precipitated them. Whether or not the changes would have occurred anyway is debatable, but it is undeniable that some of them can be traced to the Vietnam War. The Vietnam War created strains in the economy, and economic agents reacted to them, and altering the way the economy works or is perceived to work in the process.

There is no way, of course, to chart all the changes that occurred nor is it possible to understand all the implications of those changes. How many plans were altered, how many decisions postponed, how many actions were taken that would not have been necessary in other times, cannot be known. Some changes, for instance, were temporary and omitted from the foregoing discussion. There was for example, a dramatic increase in the inventory-sales ratio in 1966 as firms bumped against capacity, and the economy was booming; there was also an upsurge in direct foreign investment in the United States perhaps prompted by the same booming economy. These changes were reversed in later years but in the meantime, how many plans were altered as a result of them? Perhaps a domestic firm was discouraged from investing in its industry by the competition coming from foreign investment. There are no ready data for actions not taken.

In the end we are forced to record only those events that resulted in actions taken that were measurable. But these actions resulted in the subtle transformation of the economy and forced us to enter into uncharted areas. The old rules of the game were discarded, and the new rules were not yet available.

NOTES

1. The year 1966 was also seen as a turning point for the U.S. economy by Samuel Bowles, David M. Gordon, and Thomas E. Weisskopf in *Beyond the Waste Land* (New York: Anchor/Doubleday, 1983) and in my *U.S. National Economic Policy, 1917–1985* (New York: Praeger, 1987).

2. In the words of the Council of Economic Advisors, "A major economic accomplishment of 1966 is that the United States made essentially full use of its productive capacity. Gone were the chronic underutilization of resources, general excess supply in labor markets, and wastefully idle industrial capacity that had blemished the performance of the economy for a decade." *Economic Report of the President, 1967*, 42; later on page 74, "The year 1965 marked the end of a long period of price stability."

3. U.S. Congress, Joint Economic Committee, Wharton Econometric Forecasting Associates, "A Study in Counter-Cyclical Policy," in *Economic Stabilization Policies: the Historical Record, 1962–76*, 95th Congress, 2d Session, November 1978, 96. For the view that Vietnam War expenditures cannot be blamed for the inflation beyond 1967, see John F. Walker and Harold G. Vatter, "The Princess and the Pea; or, The Alleged Vietnam War Origins of the Current Inflation," in the *Journal of Economic Issues* 16 (June 1982): 597–608. For a contrary view see the comment to this article in the same journal by Charles B. Garrison and Anne Mayhew, "The Alleged Vietnam War Origins of the Current Inflation: A Comment," *Journal of Economic Issues* 17 (March 1983): 175–86; and the immediately following reply by Walker and Vatter, "Demonstrating the Undemonstrable: A Reply to Garrison and Mayhew," 186–96. See also the unpublished paper of Tom Riddell, "The Vietnam War and Inflation Revisited" presented at the Fifth Annual Presidential Conference Lyndon Baines Johnson: A Texan in Washington at Hofstra University, Hempstead, New York on April 10, 1986.

4. This is primarily the work of Otto Eckstein. See his *Core Inflation* (Englewood Cliffs, N.J.: Prentice-Hall, 1981).

5. Ibid., v.

6. For an excellent guide to inflation see, Robert M. Solow, "The Intelligent Citizen's Guide to Inflation," *The Public Interest* 38 (Winter 1975): 30–66.

7. John Sheahan, *The Wage-Price Guideposts* (Washington, D.C.: Brookings Institution, 1967), 90.

8. *Economic Report of the President, 1967*, 81.

9. See Okun, *The Political Economy of Prosperity* (New York: W. W. Norton, 1970), 76–78.

10. For a detailed history and development of the war on poverty see Sar A. Levitan, *The Great Society's Poor Law: A New Approach to Poverty* (Baltimore: Johns Hopkins Press, 1969). An analysis of the success of poverty programs can be found in, Robert D. Plotnick and Felicity Skidmore, *Progress Against Poverty: A Review of the 1964–1974 Decade* (New York: Academic Press, 1975).

11. For an excellent review of poverty in the United States see Isabel V. Sawhill, "Poverty in the U.S.: Why is it So Persistent?" *Journal of Economic Literature* 26 (September 1988): 1073–19.

12. Quoted by Doris Kearns, *Lyndon Johnson and the American Dream* (New York: Harper & Row, 1976), 259–60.

13. *Report of the National Advisory Commission on Civil Disorders*, chaired by Otto Kerner (Washington D.C.: Government Printing Office, March 1968), 1.

14. Levitan, *Great Society's Poor Law*, 87.

15. Martin Luther King, Jr., "Beyond Vietnam," in *Vietnam and Black America*, edited by Clyde Taylor (New York: Anchor Press/Doubleday, 1973), 81. Also in the same book, Julian Bond wrote, "The Roots of Racism and War" on page 109, about the age old divisions of rich and poor, black and white and despaired over the possibility of closing the divisions, "no nation which cares for its people can make war on another; no nation which cares about the individuality of all men could let the people of its own soil exist as some of the people of this nation do."

16. In the words of Johnson's biographer, Doris Kearns,

His [Johnson's] difficulties as a public leader were rooted in the choice he made in 1965 to commit American troops to an undeclared war in Vietnam while continuing to build the Great Society and while keeping the full extent of America's commitment from the public, the Congress, and even members of the executive branch. And taken together, these decisions produced an atmosphere of frustrated hope that contributed to the outbreaks of ugly riots in city after city for three turbulent summers.

Kearns, *Lyndon Johnson*, 303–4.

17. One of the early attempts was made by a leader in this field Edward F. Denison, "Explanations of Declining Productivity Growth," in U. S. Department of Commerce, Bureau of Economic Analysis, *Survey of Current Business* 59, no. 8 (August 1979): 1–24.

18. For the view that the decline in productivity is nonexistent and a smokescreen see "Productivity Slowdown: A False Alarm," *Monthly Review* 31 (June 1979): 1–12. The argument here is that the decline is a statistical artifact meant to provide justification for another round of speed-ups for the U.S. worker. This radical interpretation by Harry Magdoff, one of the leading Marxists in the United States was challenged by younger radicals Samuel Bowles, David Gordon, and Thomas Weisskopf, *Beyond the Waste Land* (New York: Anchor Press/Doubleday, 1983). The latter explanation for the decline in productivity involves a social determination rooted in the antagonism between labor and management.

19. Okun, *The Political Economy of Prosperity*, 71–72.

20. Walter Heller, *New Dimensions in Political Economy* (New York: W. W. Norton, 1967), 87.

21. For an excellent introduction to this fascinating idea, see Donald D. Hester, "Innovations and Monetary Control," in *Brookings Papers on Economic Activity* 1 (1981): 141–99. The discussion in the text owes much to this outstanding contribution to the literature on the efficacy of monetary policy.

22. See Bowles et al., *Beyond the Waste Land*, 84–91 for further elaboration on these points.

23. For a chronicle of labor's role in the Vietnam War, see Philip S. Foner, *American Labor and the Indochina War: The Growth of Union Opposition* (New York: International Publishers, 1971).

24. Bowles et al., *Beyond the Waste Land*, 95–97.

25. Martin Feldstein and Lawrence Summers, "Is the Rate of Profit Falling," in *Brookings Papers on Economic Activity* 1(1977): 211–28. They concluded, however, that the decline would be temporary since the fluctuations in the rate of profit, on the order of 1–2 percent were in the range of past fluctuations, and hence there was no conclusive evidence that there had been any fundamental change that would cause any permanent alterations in the rate of profit.

26. William Nordhaus, "The Falling Share of Profits," in *Brookings Papers on Economic Activity* 1 (1974): 169–217.

27. Nordhaus, 169. Without cluttering up the text, additional evidence can be found in Arthur M. Okun and George L. Perry, "Notes and Numbers on the Profits Squeeze," in *Brookings Papers on Economic Activity* 3 (1970): 466–73. They stressed the decline in productivity as a major explanation for the falling share of corporate profits.

28. U.S. Congress, Joint Economic Committee, WEFA, "A Study in Counter Cyclical Policy," 99.

5 NIXON'S WAR, 1969–73

Richard Nixon's phoenix-like return to politics found him running for the presidency in 1968. In "the speech" that varied little from delivery to delivery, Nixon promised "peace with honor" as he patted his breast giving the impression that a plan to end the war was already formulated. No plan was ever discovered, however, but Nixon won anyway as he appealed to those who were tired of paying for social programs and wanted law and order, who wanted the restoration of U.S. prestige, and who sought new leadership. Nixon presumed to speak for the silent majority although how he heard them remains a mystery.

His opponent, Vice President Hubert Humphrey, spoke of the "politics of joy" but battled despair with the albatross of the Vietnam War hanging around his neck. Threatened by Johnson with possible retaliation, he was never able or willing to disavow his support for the U.S. involvement in Southeast Asia. So instead the nation was treated to the televised spectacle of demonstrations against the war in the streets of Chicago where the Democratic presidential convention was held, and to the police riot that ensued to control the civil disobedience.

Nixon won a narrow victory in November and began the slow and imperfect turn of the society to conservative philosophy as indicated in the previous chapter. Nixon did not take the lead in transforming economic policy since he disliked economics and delegated much of the policy-making to others. Herbert Stein as chairman of the Council of Economic Advisors was one of those, and he characterized the administration as being composed of conservatives with liberal ideas.[1] All this will become evident later, but first it is necessary to review the progress of the war and Nixon's approach to it before learning how the economy was affected.

NIXON'S GAME PLANS

Nixon's secret plan turned out to be merely a variant of the bargaining through strength strategy. In this case, it meant bombing North Vietnam into negotiating (there was no hope of winning the war militarily) while solidifying the bargaining position of the United States and South Vietnam. It was his "madman theory" which was designed to throw the enemy off balance by creating the fear that his actions were both unpredictable and unconstrained. He also hoped that the Soviet Union and China could be prevailed upon to pressure the communists into agreeing to a solution of the conflict.[2]

Both avenues to peace failed as the Soviet Union remained detached except for supplying the arsenals of war. More important the bombing campaign proved remarkably unsuccessful in either destroying the war machine or the morale of the North Vietnamese. But in the process of devising the strategy, Nixon and his National Security Advisor, Henry Kissinger, had managed to centralize control over policy in the White House.

When Nixon took office in January 1969, peace talks in Paris were in progress but appeared to be going nowhere. Again resorting to force, he authorized the *secret* bombing of Cambodia in March 1969 to destroy sources of supply to the North Vietnamese. Prince Sihanouk, ruler of Cambodia, had previously informed Washington that he was not adverse to the United States crossing the border to pursue the enemy. The bombing, although exposed, was not officially admitted until 1973, but the invasion into Cambodia in April 1970 was more difficult to hide. The war was becoming "Nixon's war" without question.

Meanwhile under pressure from the public, Congress, and members of his own administration, Nixon began to withdraw troops from Vietnam. In June of 1969, 25,000 troops were repatriated. This was part of the game plan called "Vietnamization" in which South Vietnamese troops were to be substituted for U.S. troops. The general policy, announced first in July 1969, of sending arms rather than men where deemed necessary, quickly became known as the Nixon Doctrine.

The policy of withdrawing troops while negotiating for peace is, of course, inconsistent since the North had only to wait out the troop withdrawals to achieve its objectives. The North was in no hurry, but the U.S. was under increasing pressure to reduce its involvement in Southeast Asia. Indeed many in Congress were proposing legislation to fix various dates for the total withdrawal of troops. Accordingly, periodic troop withdrawals were made as shown in Table 5.1. As these troop withdrawals were taking place, Kissinger began secret peace talks in August 1969 in Paris with the North Vietnamese. As was typical of an administration that valued secrecy and surprise, these talks were not revealed until January 1972.

The war dragged on, of course, despite rumors of peace. In October 1972, just prior to national elections, Kissinger announced a breakthrough in the Paris talks. However the "peace is at hand" condition broke down, and the bombing of the North was resumed on Christmas day to bring the North back to the negotiating table. The North Vietnamese agreed to talk after the bombing stopped, and eventually a peace agreement was reached in Paris in January 1973. The hated draft was ended, and the last troops left Vietnam in March.

This very brief summary was included only to review some of the more important events and dates and to prepare for the discussion of what was occurring in the economy at the same time. First, let us review the immediate costs of the war in dollar terms and reserve other costs for later discussion.

THE DOMESTIC SCENE

The troop withdrawals and the slow winding down of the war did not appease the critics of U.S. involvement in Southeast Asia. Even after the

Table 5.1
Vietnam Troop Withdrawals

Date of Announcement	Number	New Limit
		549,500 a
June 8, 1969	25,000	524,500
Sept. 19, 1969	40,500	484,000
Dec. 15, 1969	50,000	434,000
Apr. 20, 1970	150,000	284,000
Apr. 7, 1971	100,000	184,000
Nov. 12, 1971	45,000	139,000
Jan. 13, 1972	70,000	69,000
Apr. 26, 1972	20,000	49,000
June 28, 1972	10,000	39,000

[a] Ceiling prior to June 8, 1969.

Source: U.S. Department of Defense (Comptroller), *The Economics of Defense Spending: A Look at the Realities* (Washington, D.C.: Government Printing Office, July 1972), 149.

first two troop reductions, there were massive antiwar demonstrations in Washington—one in October and one in November 1969. Earlier, the revelation that hundreds of innocent villagers had been massacred in My-Lai in 1968 inflamed many, and the knowledge that this was only an extreme case of common practices sent shudders among both opponents and advocates of the war. The nation became preoccupied with the war, a war that just would not recede into the background and permit people to go about their daily business. In fact the war became a poison that spread into the bloodstream of the nation as it was being consumed by it. The universities were in turmoil as faculty and students protested U.S. policies; households were divided over the justification for the war; friends were pitted against each other; political parties became factious, and so on. No one appeared immune to the infection.

Following the invasion into Cambodia, the demonstrations began anew, and in May, four students were killed at Kent State by national guardsmen. Once again the nation was shocked by the apparent senselessness of the slaying and by the spectacle of troops on a college campus. The headlines reflected the shame and bewilderment of the confused public. It was not a good time for apathy.

The demonstrations trailed off as more and more troops were withdrawn and U.S. direct involvement appeared to diminish. Eventually the war was turned over to the South Vietnamese and they proceeded to blunder themselves into defeat; in April 1975 the war was over and the North had won, but in the process Cambodia fell to the communists as well.

Before updating the costs of the war, it would be appropriate to reiterate a note of warning. It might be possible to document the direct costs of the war, and even here the difficulties are formidable, but to attempt to account for the social costs of the war is virtually impossible. There simply is no calculus to enable us to identify and add together the social costs that this unpopular war inflicted on the American public. Honest young men learned to lie to escape the draft, learned to enter into careers or career paths that would enable them to avoid military service, or learned that to flee was the best avenue of escape. Families were devastated or broken by such decisions and even middle and upper-class families learned that merely paying the defense bill was not sufficient and began to object when their sons were made subject to the draft. The poor learned, if they did not know it before, that they were expendable. Since the war was so pervasive, nearly every decision, whether it be an occupational one or not, was affected by the impact of the war. It would be impossible to list all the decisions affected by the war, every choice made with it in the background, or each problem caused by the war that forced a decision that would otherwise have been unnecessary. All that we can do is to note the omission in passing and lament the lack of a calculus that would permit more searching analysis of social costs.

DIRECT MILITARY COSTS

The direct military costs are less intangible than social costs although by no means as accurate as one would like or expect. Table 5.2 provides the estimates for the entire involvement in Vietnam.

The official direct cost of the war according to the Office of Budget and Management (OMB) was $140 billion, which places it second in expense to World War II which had a cost of $360 billion. These numbers do not

Table 5.2
Estimates of Expenditures on Vietnam War (Fiscal Year; in Billions of Dollars)

Year	Actual Total Costs	Incremental Costs	Brookings
1965	$ 0.1	$ 0.1	$ –
1966	5.8	5.8	–
1967	20.1	18.4	–
1968	26.5	20.0	24.1
1969	28.8	21.5	24.2
1970	23.0	17.4	16.7
1971	14.7	11.5	11.0
1972	9.4	7.0	6.8
1973	6.3	4.5	3.5
1974	3.1	–	–
1975	1.4	–	–
1976	0.3	–	–
Total	139.5	–	–

Notes: Full costs are all the official costs of operations in the war; incremental costs are all official costs over and above what would have been incurred anyway by regular base line forces— i.e., the amounts that could be removed from the budget without the war.

Sources: Actual costs are those of the Office of Management and Budget and are taken from U.S. House of Representatives, Committee on the Budget, *Chronology of Major Fiscal and Monetary Policies (1960–1977)*, prepared by the Task Force on Economic Policy (Washington, D.C.: U.S. Government Printing Office, January 1978), 197; The Brookings data included in the report were taken originally from *Setting National Priorities, the 1973 Budget* (Washington, D.C.: Brookings Institution, 1972), 75; Incremental costs from U.S. Department of Defense (Comptroller), *The Economics of Defense Spending* (Washington, D.C.: U.S. Government Printing Office, July 1972), 149. The incremental costs for 1972 and 1973 were estimated by the author by interpolation of published data.

appear very large with respect to the amounts spent on national defense in the 1980s that were approximately $300 billion. However in terms of the spending on national defense in the 1960s, which were on the order of $75–80 billion, they are large indeed. For example, in 1968, the expenditures on the Vietnam War represented approximately 34 percent of all defense spending and in 1969 the proportion rose to 37 percent. Put in this relationship, the expenditures made in Vietnam are substantial and cannot be dismissed as insignificant either as to their effects on the defense budget or on the economy.

Moreover there has always been a question as to whether the costs were recorded accurately to reflect the true costs of waging the war. Clearly understating the costs of the war would serve many purposes: an unpopular war would not appear to cost as much in monetary terms and taxes that went to support it would not be as painful; the peace dividend, the amounts promised to be returned to the civilian economy once the war ended, would be smaller; and the effects of military spending on the economy and the society would be minimized.

The total costs could be understated in many ways, not all of them readily observable. If one were interested in the full costs of the Vietnam War, it would be necessary to adjust the totals of Table 5.2 to account for unrecorded costs. One such attempt was made by Robert W. Stevens who, for example, made a $15 billion addition for the failure of the Defense Department to include the full costs of military personnel.[3] (This correction made by Stevens and other adjustments will be discussed in Chapter 6.) However, these estimates are not precise or even entirely justified, and the true costs of military personnel, both those directly involved and in support roles, can never be known with any degree of accuracy. Since we are not primarily interested in accounting for the "true" costs of the war, the issue can be put aside until Chapter 6 as we return to the main concern—the domestic economic consequences of the war.

THE ECONOMY IN THE NIXON YEARS

The Nixon administrations brought to Washington the conservative economics that had been growing in influence during the Kennedy-Johnson years. As noted in the last chapter, they included: the rejection of fiscal policy; the reliance on controlling the growth of money, even to establishing a fixed rate of growth of the money supply; the belief in free and unregulated markets; and the need for a balanced budget. The Nixon economists, however, were not dogmatic conservatives and did not rigidly subscribe to all of these beliefs.

Accordingly when they began to construct macroeconomic policy, they were more pragmatic. Still the problem of inflation, a traditional issue for conservatives, soon became the priority concern. Unfortunately, past efforts to combat inflation usually involved "root canal economics" whereby recessions were required to control inflation. But recessions cause unemployment, and Nixon was sensitive to the unemployment issue since he claimed that the failure to confront the unemployment problem in 1960 cost him the presidential election.

When Nixon took office in January 1969, the unemployment rate was 3.6 percent and the CPI was rising at an annual rate of approximately 4.5 percent. The problem for the administration was how to reduce the rate of inflation without raising the unemployment rate above the (now) socially acceptable rate of 4 percent. The guideposts, the concept a victim of the war, were discredited, and any other type of direct intervention into the economy was out in the free market atmosphere of this administration. So the administration adopted a policy of "gradualism" that was an attempt to cool off the economy over a longer time period with the primary means of restraint coming from the monetary side.

Thus the growth of the money supply slowed from 7.2 percent in 1968 to 2.5 percent in 1969 for the year as a whole, but in the latter half of the year the rate of growth fell to only 0.7 percent. The discount rate was also increased in April to indicate even more directly the movement toward monetary restraint. Fiscal policy also moved toward restraint as expenditures were cut by $7.5 billion and the budget registered a small surplus of $3.2 billion (but an $11.7 billion surplus in the high employment budget from a deficit of $6.0 billion in 1968).

The gradualism policy, however, did not work. Monetary restraint drove interest rates up to their highest levels since the Civil War with three-month Treasury Bills at 7.7 percent in December and mortgage rates at 8.5 percent; another credit crunch was in the making. Once again, the demand for funds was strong resulting in the withdrawal of funds from institutions with interest rate ceilings. Banks turned to other sources of funds: Eurodollars, repurchase agreements, bank holding companies, etc., as outlined in the last chapter. Financial flows were altered with favored customers securing funds but with the housing market declining. So in the effort to control inflation, monetary restraint was instead creating the conditions wherein market participants were finding ways around the restraint and in the process altering the financial structure of the economy. In the future, monetary policy would be less effective as a result of the new institutions springing into place to avoid the consequences of the Federal Reserve's policies. [4]

Again the inflation caused by the Vietnam War was changing the structure of the economy. If that were not sufficient, inflationary expectations were being allowed to develop, and high interest rates did not curtail spending. The high costs of borrowing could easily be met by the higher returns caused by inflation. The inflationary psychology, as it came to be called, soon was built into the plans of everyone and once begun is difficult to reverse.

The Tax Reform Act of 1969, passed over the objections of the administration, also potentially modified the structure of the economic system away from fixed investment by removing the investment tax credit, reducing accelerated depreciation allowances, curtailing depletion allowances, and increasing the taxation of capital gains. The immediate aim of reducing inflation could have been at the expense of long-term growth, and even though investment showed remarkable strength in 1969 considering the announced attempts to restrain it, the longer-term prospects were doubtful.

The results of the policy of gradualism were disappointing indeed. The GNP fell in a mini recession, from a growth rate of 4.9 percent in the previous year to 2.8 percent in 1969. Unemployment fell slightly to 3.5 percent while prices rose—by 5.4 percent in the CPI (from 4.2 percent), by 3.9 percent in the WPI (from 2.4 percent), and by 4.7 percent in the GNP price index (from 4.0 percent). Meanwhile two million people were added to the ranks of the employed, mainly women and teens and many at part time jobs, but the productivity of labor showed no increase while wage and fringe benefits were rising at a 7–8 percent rate. Clearly there were signs of trouble ahead, and the administration was not preparing for it, but in fact promising more of the same.

The tight labor market and rising inflation brought many women into the labor force, a trend that would affect the society in many ways not fully recognized at the time. The effects on family life, the structure of jobs, the need for facilities for the care of children, etc., were yet to be given serious consideration. The entrance of women and teens into the labor force was also identified as one of the causes of the continued decline in the productivity growth of labor. The rapid entrance into the labor force of young people of the baby boom generation, and the growth in labor force participation of women, accounted for a reduction of 0.4 percentage point in the annual growth rate of productivity in the period 1965 to 1973. The Council of Economic Advisors, who made that estimate, also concluded that the rate of reduction had fallen to 0.33 of a percentage point after that period.[5] With even more experience, the decline in the growth of productivity from this source would no longer be as dramatic.

ECONOMIC POLICY REVERSALS

The policy of gradualism eventually led the economy into a mild recession that began in December 1969 and lasted until November 1970. But as the GNP fell slightly, the unemployment rate rose, and stagflation became a reality. (See Table 5.3 for details.) The monetary authorities reversed their tight money policy and permitted the money supply to grow 5.4 percent for the year. The credit crunch was eased. Interest rates fell slightly but the financial markets were shaken by several events: the invasion into Cambodia followed by the incident at Kent State and the collapse of Penn Central Railroad.

In May, following the Cambodian invasion, the stock market fell by about 15 percent from the first of the year, remained sluggish through the summer, but recovered by the end of the year. The collapse of Penn Central created immediate fears of a liquidity crisis. Since the credit crunch of 1966, corporations seeking to avoid a similar crisis, began to raise funds by selling commercial paper. When they became due the firms simply rolled them over and little notice was taken of financial soundness. When Penn Central could not repay its loans, concern for the ability of other firms to repay theirs arose, and of course, restricted the ability of corporations to raise additional funds in this manner. The liquidity crisis was becoming real for the banks were loaned up, and the stock market was depressed.

Once again the credit crunch of 1966 was affecting the economy as shown in the last chapter. Now the second credit crunch of 1969 was bringing the economy close to another genuine liquidity crisis. Again banks and corporations reacted to the previous credit crunches by seeking avenues to protect themselves but now those avenues were partially blocked as well. Moreover the fears of a liquidity crisis were heightened by the rumors of possible collapses of major U.S. corporations—Lockheed and Chrysler among them. In September, several brokerage houses were also facing bankruptcy when mismanagement of the operations resulted in millions of dollars of securities being lost. The volume of transactions could not be handled even by computers.

Thus the Federal Reserve had to react, and it did so by opening the discount window so that banks could make loans. The liquidity crisis and possible panic were averted. Clearly, however, the concern for inflation had to be relaxed. The ability to fight inflation was now being hampered by the very institutions that were set up in response to past efforts to fight inflation.

The administration continued to cling to the belief that proper macro-economic policies could be employed to bring the inflation rate down to

Table 5.3
Selected Economic Series, 1969–74 (Percent Change Except Where Noted; Quarterly Data at Annual Rates)

Year & Quarter	GNP			Prices			Unemploy Rate	Mfg. Operating Capacity
	GNP	National Defense Purchases	GNP (in 1958$)	CPI (1957–59=100)	WPI	GNP Index (1958=100)	(%)	(%)
1969	7.6	0.1	2.7	6.1	4.8	4.8	3.9	90.0
1970	5.0	-4.8	-0.4	5.5	2.2	5.5	5.3	86.2
1971	8.0	-4.0	3.3	3.4	4.0	4.5	6.4	85.3
1971 I	15.0	-0.8	7.9	2.4	7.4	5.9	5.9	86.4
II	7.9	-1.4	3.4	5.8	4.7	4.4	6.0	87.3
III	6.5	-1.4	2.7	2.3	0.7	2.9	6.0	83.2
IV	8.0	3.0	6.1	3.0	3.2	1.5	5.9	84.3
1972	9.8	5.0	6.2	3.4	6.5	3.4	6.0	89.6
1973	11.8	-0.5	5.9	8.8	15.4	5.6	5.2	93.0
1974	7.9	5.6	-2.2	12.2	20.9	10.2	6.1	87.4

Source: Economic Reports of the President, 1972–1975 (Washington, D.C.: Government Printing Office).

the 3 percent range and the unemployment rate down to 4.5 percent range by mid-1972—just in time for the next election. But the real world did not cooperate, and both the inflation and unemployment rates were above these targets in mid-1971. The administration, led by Secretary of the Treasury John Connally, decided to apply a shock treatment to the economy at this time in order to get closer to the targets before the election and before accusations of political manipulation of the economy could be leveled. So it embarked on August 15, 1971 on the most anticapitalist policy that could be devised—wage and price controls—a policy that implies that the free market is not working. For a group of allegedly conservative economists, this was drastic medicine and only showed the lengths to which the administration was willing to go to win the election (the Watergate scandal was another).

Yet the economic data hardly justified such draconian measures. Even a quick examination of Table 5.3 is sufficient to reveal that economic conditions were far from catastrophic. The unemployment rate was hovering around 6 percent, and the CPI was rising at just over 5 percent in the second quarter of 1971. Here was Nixon who had disavowed the use of controls, but who loved to govern by surprise, proposing dramatic actions and looking decisive and presidential in the process.[6]

One cannot attribute the policy of wage and price controls directly to the Vietnam War, but it is possible to suggest that the policy reactions to past problems had not worked, and some of these problems did emanate from the war. Gradualism and credit crunches were ineffective as policy moves and more drastic actions were required regardless of ideological conflicts. Politics, pragmatism, and problems in the international economy won out over ideological purity.

The controls were in effect until April 1973, and while the debate over their economic effectiveness continues to the present, there is no debate about whether or not they helped reelect Nixon for a second term. After the election, the administration's interest in controls quickly waned both because they had done their job, and because other concerns began to overwhelm the administration. The Watergate affair and the Arab oil embargo began to occupy the nation as well as the economic policymakers. Anyway it was no great feat to declare that the controls were not working, not desirable, and not necessary any longer. Yet looking at the data in Table 5.3 reveals that the controls did serve to moderate the rate of increase in prices but they also created many stains in the economic system such that when they were removed, prices rose rapidly. Evidence suggests that the controls were ill-designed and ill-administered, but whether the controls worked or not is not the issue here; the point is that they were employed after a series of inappropriate policies at least in part attributable to problems created by the Vietnam War.[7]

In the end the controls program was a political not an economic policy and should more properly be judged on that basis. It allowed the administration to pursue expansionary monetary and fiscal policies without worrying about the consequences for inflation. A booming economy is very useful in an election campaign, and that is what the administration wanted and got. After the election was won, it could revert to more traditional policy-making to repair whatever damages were inflicted on the public and the economy. Thus in 1972 the administration urged federal agencies to spend, spend, spend, and if a higher deficit resulted, it could be corrected over time. This expansionary fiscal policy, designed to stimulate the economy just prior to the election, was matched by an expansionary monetary policy to facilitate the stimulative fiscal policy. Arthur Burns, chairman of the Federal Reserve Board, was pressured to pursue an easy money policy, and he caved in and supplied the necessary monetary expansion.

After the election both monetary and fiscal policy turned restrictive, and late in 1973 the economy turned down into another recession. This is yet another example of political business cycles in which political rather than economic considerations were dominant in determining the direction of the economy.[8] These are intriguing developments in economic policy-making, but they cannot be discussed in detail here and divert us away from determining the economic consequences of the Vietnam War. In January 1973 peace agreements had been signed, the draft was ended, and in March the last of the U.S. troops had been removed from Vietnam.

While expenditures identified with the war continued, they only amounted to about $5 billion, hardly large enough to affect an economy with a GNP of $1.3 trillion dollars. So Nixon's war ended to be followed by the Watergate revelations and the oil embargo. Nixon's attention to economic affairs, never high on his list of exciting problems, now fell to nil, and his aides were given even more responsibility for economic policy-making. The Watergate affair consumed him, and eventually drove him from office in 1974. Nixon finally achieved peace but not with honor.

NOTES

1. Herbert Stein, *Presidential Economics* (New York: Simon & Schuster, 1984), 133.

2. For more historical background, see Stanley Karnow, *Vietnam: A History* (New York: Viking Press, 1983), 582–600.

3. Robert Warren Stevens, *Vain Hopes, Grim Realities* (New York: New Viewpoints, 1976), 95–102.

4. For an interesting analysis of the role of credit crunches, see Albert M. Wojnilower, "The Central Role of Credit Crunches in Recent Financial History," *Brookings Papers on Economic Activity* 2 (1980): 277–337.

5. Council of Economic Advisors, *Economic Report of the President, 1979*, 68.

6. For an intimate look at the formation of the controls policy, see Stein, *Presidential Economics*.

7. Many attempts have been made to determine the efficacy of wage and price controls. Among them are the discussion papers on the panel, "Two Years of Wage-Price Controls," that appeared in the *American Economic Review* 64 (May 1974): 82–104; and Karl Brunner and Alan Meltzer, eds., *The Economics of Price and Wage Controls*, vol. 2 (Amsterdam: Carnegie-Rochester Conference Series, 1976). See also Anthony S. Campagna, *U.S. National Economic Policies, 1917–1985* (New York: Praeger, 1987), 376–96.

8. For confirmation of this political business cycle, see Douglas A. Hibbs, Jr., *The American Political Economy: Macroeconomics and Electoral Politics* (Cambridge, Mass.: Harvard University Press, 1987), 264–65. It is difficult to quarrel with his observation that "without the 1972 experience to stimulate interest in the topic, it is doubtful that most of the subsequent writing about the political business cycle phenomenon ever would have appeared."

III The Economic and Societal Consequences of the Vietnam War: A Final Accounting

6 ECONOMIC COSTS AND BENEFITS OF THE WAR

The discussion of the economic consequences of the Vietnam War up to this point has proceeded according to how the macroeconomy was affected. Some of the effects of the war were easily seen, e.g., the effects of inflation, and were relatively uncontroversial. But the analysis did not go far enough and did not capture the full economic costs of the war. It is time for a full accounting. One would like to write "final" accounting but the total costs of the war will never be known. Still a more comprehensive definition of the costs as well as benefits is required for a better, if incomplete, accounting.

Several studies have made estimates of the economic costs of the Vietnam War; some of these have already been mentioned but others not previously cited must now be considered. While all of them did not undertake a full accounting over the entire course of the war, they all recognized that the full economic costs would include the following:

—The actual budgetary costs of the war

—Future budgetary costs that will be incurred as a result of the war

—Unrecorded and hence unrecognized economic costs of the war

—Indirect costs that can be reasonably imputed to the war

ACTUAL BUDGETARY COSTS

The actual budgetary costs of the war are easiest to define and record. Although not without controversy, these costs are recognized in official sources. Table 6.1 summarizes some of these identifiable costs.

Table 6.1
Actual Budgetary Costs of the War (in Billions of Dollars)

I. Direct Costs, 1965-1976	
A. Direct costs per	
1. Office of Management and Budget (Table 5.2) and Department of Defense[a]	$ 136.6
2. Adjustments to Full costs for failure of DOD to account for full personnel costs and understatement of full costs in 1965-67[b]	15.0
3. Direct Personnel Costs prior to 1965[c]	.8
4. U.S. Military Aid to:	
France and emperor Bao Dai, 1950-54[d]	2.5-3.0
Laos and Thailand, 1950-66[e]	.9
Cambodia, 1950-76[e]	1.3
South Vietnam, 1953-65[f]	2.4
5. U.S. Economic Aid to Indochina and So. Vietnam, 1950-76[g]	9.4
6. Support for the Free World Military Assistance Forces- So. Korea, Philippines, Thailand, 1965-69[h]	1.3
7. CIA Funds used to Support U.S. Policy[i]	n/a
Estimated Total Direct Costs[j]	$ 173.2

[a] Department of Defense data were preliminary for the years 1972 on so the estimates were adjusted for the years 1972–76 in the above.

[b] Calculations made by Robert W. Stevens in *Vain Hopes, Grim Realities* (New York: New Viewpoints, 1976), 95–98.

[c] Calculations made by Murray Wiedenbaum in *Economic Impact of the Vietnam War*, Center for Strategic Studies, Special Report Series No. 5, Georgetown University (Washington, D.C.: Renaissance Editions, 1967), 21.

[d] Stanley Karnow, *Vietnam: A History* (New York: Viking Press, 1983), 137, 177.

[e] Department of Defense, *Foreign Military Sales and Military Assistance Facts*, December 1976.

[f] Major General L. B. Taylor, *Financial Management of the Vietnam Conflict, 1962–1972* (Washington D.C., Department of the Army, 1974), 23.

[g] U.S. *Statistical Abstract*, 1977, 363.

[h] United States Senate, Committee on Foreign Relations, Subcommittee on *United States Security Agreements and Commitments Abroad, part 1, Republic of Philippines*, 91st Congress, 1st session, September and October, 1969, 96, 358; part 3, *Kingdom of Thailand*. November 1969, 657; part 6, *Republic of Korea*, 91st Congress, 2d session, February 1970, 1545.

[i] Stanley Karnow in *Vietnam* (New York: Viking Press, 1983), frequently mentions the CIA and the use of funds but no sources are given for these assertions.

[j] Clearly these are rather crude estimates since much of the data are still classified or Vietnam expenditures have not been separated from more general budgetary totals.

Items 1 through 3 of Table 6.1 do not require much explanation. Yet the official estimated costs of the war have always been questioned, sometimes encouraged by the reporting of them. Reporting full costs in some periods and incremental costs in another only increased the suspicion that the numbers were being manipulated for political purposes.

One underestimation of full costs is seldom mentioned but illustrates the reason for continued skepticism. Equipment, planes, tanks, etc.,used in the war from stock were not counted as costs. Only material purchased for Vietnam were included as costs.[1] Clearly the amounts involved could be enormous.

But we can ask: Why did the war cost so much? The answer from one analyst is straightforward. Thomas Thayer states, "The answer lies in the way we chose to fight the war—American Style, with our most expensive forces. . . . It was, in resource allocation terms, first and foremost an air war, and second, a ground attrition campaign against VC/NVA regular units. Pacification was a very poor third."[2]

Item 2, the understatement of full costs arises because in the early years of the war, the Department of Defense (DOD) did not make any estimates (or underestimated them) for the full costs of the personnel in Southeast Asia. Only incremental personnel costs were counted. However, it is well recognized that for every member of the armed forces directly involved there is some multiple of that number needed in support—i.e. a 1.5:1 or 2:1 ratio. Stevens estimated an additional $15 billion adjustment for the full personnel costs of the war: $7 billion of which is due to the nonrecognition of full personnel costs over the period 1965–72; and $7.5 billion is due to the underestimation of the official full personnel cost for fiscal years 1966 and 1967.[3]

U.S. military aid (Item 4) is self explanatory but is by no means uncontroversial. The amounts given to France in the early 1950s are not well documented. Moreover other military aid might have been given in the absence of hostilities as part of the SEATO arrangements. The same is true of economic aid to the region. Some of the aid might have been forthcoming whether or not the United States was seeking allies or trying to avert the spread of the war into other nations. However it is still justifiable to consider the bulk of economic aid as motivated by the need to retain control or influence over the other nations contiguous to the conflict.

In the attempt to justify the intervention into Vietnam and to demonstrate the dangers in the region, the United States sought to bring other nations into supporting its policy. The United Nations and many nations were called upon to support the actions of the United States, and a few finally responded with military support—the Philippines, Korea, Thailand, Australia, New Zealand. The administration claimed that these nations were willing to supply combat troops and support and were motivated by the desire to aid in the noble cause of stopping the spread of communism in Southeast Asia. Australia and New Zealand provided only token support, but even this was questioned in their own nations. The other countries were little more than mercenaries since the United States made some very beneficial agreements that allowed them to profit from this alliance.

For instance, in an elaborate agreement with South Korea, the United States agreed to pay all the costs of deployment of troops and supporting elements. Korean troops were paid an overseas allowance that amounted to as much as their regular salaries, i.e., they were paid double their normal pay. In addition the United States agreed to buy from Korean suppliers the requirements of their forces and agreed to help them develop their export markets. (In the 1980s when imports from South Korea flooded U.S. markets this would appear to have been the height of folly.) Moreover economic aid was promised, and an unspecified amount of loans was included in the agreement. This kind of agreement was kept secret from the American public, but in the hearings of the Senate Foreign Relations Committee, Senator Fulbright suggested that instead of Koreans making a noble sacrifice in joining forces with the United States, they were simply making a good business deal.[4]

Other nations contributed token humanitarian aid or relief supplies. Spain, for example, contributed a medical team, and Taiwan sent an agricultural team, a psychological warfare team, an electrical power mission, and a surgical team.[5] Most were being careful not to alienate a powerful ally. In other areas, the United States was training or employing other mercenaries, the Montagnards, to fight in Laos, Cambodia, or anywhere in Indochina. Getting Asians to fight other Asians was an old French scheme, and preceded the Nixon's policy of Vietnamization that was championed in the 1970s.[6]

Finally the CIA was involved in all phases of the war, from its inception to the end. It used its funds to secure cooperation, to finance operations before they were legitimized, and to buy the compliance of officials to adhere to U.S. goals. Unfortunately the budgets of the CIA are not made public and no estimate of these amounts is possible. Item 7 is included in Table 6.1 to remind us that some of the costs of the conflict can never be accounted for and to raise questions about a policy that permitted such unaccountability.

FUTURE BUDGETARY COSTS

Difficult as they are to estimate, direct budgetary war costs are easily understood. Yet the costs of the war do not end when the war is terminated.

In the United States it has always been deemed appropriate to compensate veterans for the sacrifices they made and in fact the compensation has gotten more and more generous each time they are reconsidered. But the interesting part is that the costs of veterans' benefits extends over many years after the war is over, and consequently the total costs involved are much more than the direct costs of the war. When benefits paid to dependents are included, it is even more dramatic and may extend to as much as 100 years after the war was concluded.[7]

Clearly estimating total veterans' benefits would seem impossible and a hopeless exercise to be undertaken by those who retain an interest in puzzles. Not only do the benefits change but the proportion of those who avail themselves of them changes as well. About all that can be done is to review the record of past wars and compute the percentage of the original war costs and apply that percentage to the costs of the Vietnam War. James L. Clayton has been making such estimates for some time and has come up with the following for the last two wars (the experience of earlier wars, while interesting, does not appear to be useful since the benefits, public attitudes, and proportions of those who utilize the benefits can be expected to have changed significantly): for World War II, veterans' benefits are 101 percent of the original cost and for the Korean War, 184 percent.[8] In estimating the future costs, Clayton used the latter percentage as the appropriate one. Applying that average, 184 percent, to the approximate budgetary cost of the Vietnam War, $155 billion, yields a future budgetary cost of $285 billion; applying an average, 142 percent, of these two wars yields a future budgetary cost of $220 billion. (See Table 6.2.)

These are staggering sums and difficult to put in perspective, but in 1984 both would have exceeded all the income that flowed to black and hispanic households. But the story of future costs does not stop there, for future interest costs must also be considered. Again the future interest payments on debt incurred to fight the war are nearly impossible to isolate. Not only is debt incurred for other reasons but the past debt is never repaid. Thus World War II debt is still earning interest on bonds that have not been

Table 6.2
Future Budgetary Costs (In Billions of Dollars)

Veteran's Benefits	$ 220
Interest Costs	31
Total	$ 251

redeemed but rolled over. As a consequence, interest costs for World War II and the Korean War cannot be calculated. Interest costs for World War I were calculated at about 42 percent of the original cost.[9] Still there is no way to compare the financing of the Vietnam War to World War I; the two wars are far too different in every way. Yet to ignore interest costs because they cannot be accurately measured is to understate the total costs associated with the war. The interest costs of earlier wars ranged from 15 percent in the Spanish-American War to 37 percent in the Civil War (Union only). Thus if the past is any guide, a risky assumption, the interest costs for the Vietnam War could range from 14–42 percent. Clayton suggests a percentage at least as large as 20 percent for the Vietnam War, and it is that proportion that will be used here.[10]

Applying 20 percent to the approximate cost of the Vietnam War yields a total future interest cost of $31 billion. It should be understood that interest costs, unlike some of the other costs, do not necessarily represent a burden to the community since interest payments represent a transfer to bondholders from taxpayers. (Similarly other transfer, like payments to survivors, are also not a burden to the entire community.) There may be some adverse redistribution effects of the transfer but no loss of income to the nation. In this period most of the bonds were held internally, however the future burden of these interest costs may change as more foreigners hold the old bonds as assets.

Budgetary costs, either present or future, present estimation difficulties but are easily comprehended. They are direct costs that were induced by and can reasonably be attributed to the war. But the war imposes other costs to those who are forced to alter their plans as a direct result of the war. Some of the interrupted or altered plans, such as postponed marriages, may not be important enough to consider attempting cost estimates, or the costs may be too small to worry about. However much they disrupt the lives of the individuals involved, the costs to society may not be worth the effort or be too difficult to compute.

However there are some costs to individuals that are significant and should be included in any attempt to account for the total costs of the war. Those who served directly in the war were forced to incur costs that were not imposed on the rest of the community. As the war called for increasing numbers of troops, the government conscripted large numbers of individuals and in so doing subjected them to a special kind of taxation that others were not obligated to pay. This conscription tax is roughly the difference between what the individual was paid as a member of the armed forces and what he would have been paid as a civilian employee. This is a discriminatory tax since those who did not enter the armed forces did not pay the tax and only through coercion can such a tax be imposed.

The conscription tax applies to those who were drafted or those who volunteered under the threat of induction. In the Vietnam War, however, not everyone was required to serve in the armed forces and for some time, certain groups were excluded altogether, e.g., college students. Thus not only did the threat of induction fall disproportionally on the low-income, uneducated members of the society, but conditions were set up to provide incentives for others to evade the draft. Hence in addition to the conscription tax itself, it was necessary to incur costs to collect the tax. In the words of Robert Eisner:

How many hundreds of thousands of young men have been wasting years educational resources which they do not want and do not use, because they find this the most effective means of avoiding service in a war of which they want no part? How many young men have been forced into idleness or temporary jobs because employers would not hire them in view of the possible imminence of military service? How many indeed have left the economy by literally hiding from the draft, fleeing the country or going to prison?[11]

Both costs should be recognized as part of the economic costs of the war, and several attempts have been made to estimate these losses to society. The justification for and the procedures involved in making such estimates were made by Larry Sjaastad, "Conscription as a Tax," Chapter 3 of *The Report of the President's Commission on an All-Volunteer Armed Force*.[12] Using these procedures, Robert Eisner estimated the costs of the draft at $76 billion for fiscal years 1966–1970.[13] The Cornell University Air War Study Group, using slightly updated data found the costs to be $60 billion for fiscal years 1966–71.[14] Finally Robert Stevens made his own estimate using only the difference in earnings as the cost of conscription and came up with $15 billion for the years 1965–72.[15]

All are careful to warn of the difficulties of making such estimates, and their works should be consulted by the interested reader. Moreover, all have concluded that their estimates are on the conservative side. However since the Cornell Group included tax collection costs and used updated data from earlier studies, its estimate of $60 billion will be used here.

Finally there is to be considered the loss of output from the men who were killed or hospitalized. In the case of those killed in action, their productivity over their lifetime is lost forever; whatever they may have

Table 6.3
Some Economic Costs of the War (in Billions of Dollars)

Conscription Tax	$ 60
Earnings Loss of Casualties	23
Total	$ 83

contributed to the nation is sacrificed. One cannot measure the lost music, paintings, or contributions to science, of course, but it is possible to estimate the value of their lost output by examining the earnings sacrificed and using this as a rough guide. Using data developed by Eisner, the average annual earnings of males 20 and over in 1969 was approximately $10,000. If 40 years is used as an estimate of their working lives, and the number killed was 57,777, the total earnings loss is $ 23 billion.[16] Some of the earnings would have been used to support themselves and should be deducted but since no growth in the earnings is allowed ($10,000 is used throughout), and no estimate is made regarding the earnings loss of the disabled or hospitalized, the unadjusted loss of $23 billion is used here.[17] Table 6.3 summarizes the economic costs.

OTHER COSTS

With the amount of inflation over the period, it might be expected that the U.S. balance of payments would be adversely affected. Unless our inflation were matched by our trading partners, our export prices would make selling abroad difficult. In addition, rapid inflation and tight labor markets might also cause supply or bottleneck problems, and these supply problems could put U.S. manufacturers at a disadvantage in world markets.

Wartime conditions cause additional problems for foreign trade. In a wartime situation, direct purchases of food, services and the like from foreign countries for the military are routine, but they add to the balance of payments problem. Similarly, it is usually the case that more inputs are purchased from foreigners to be used as inputs in defense production, again adversely affecting trade balances.

While these possible adverse trade conditions are readily acknowledged, the difficulty of estimating them is troublesome: how do you separate the effects of the war from what might have occurred in its absence? One attempt was made by Leonard Dudley and Peter Passell.[18] For the period 1964–67, they found that the U.S. current account balance had been adversely affected by some $4 billion. The current account balance measures the net balances of merchandise trade, the net investment income, net travel balances, and other services. Of the $4 billion, $1.6 billion was accounted for by direct foreign purchases; $1.1 billion by purchases of inputs from abroad; and $1.3 billion by the indirect effects of the decline in exports.

These are large numbers and account for most of the deterioration in the U.S. current account balance over the period. For 1964, the current account balance was + $5.8 billion; thereafter it fell steadily to + $4.3 billion in 1965, + $2.3 billion in 1966, and to + $2.1 billion in 1967. (The current account balance never did recover to prewar amounts for the duration of the war.) Since the accumulated decline from 1964 to 1967 nearly matches the total decline that Dudley and Passell attribute to the Vietnam War, there must have been an underlying trend of improvement in the balance of payments to offset this decline. In the absence of the war, trade balances should have been improving.

Looking at the simulation studies of the last chapter supports this contention. In either model, net exports (exports minus imports) would have been greater had there been no war. The OMB model shows an increase of $9.3 billion in net exports over the period 1966–67, and the WEFA model shows an increase of $3.8 billion.

The loss appears to be plausible but how much remains the question.[19] Stevens adjusted Dudley and Passell's data by the WPI to arrive at a total through 1972 of $48 billion. [20] The basis for this type of adjustment is not clear and was not explained or justified. A more reasonable, although no more defensible, estimate would be to accept the WEFA results and extend them for the balance of the war. This would make the total loss of net exports about $7.6 billion through 1973. (A similar extrapolation of Dudley and Passell's estimate would be approximately $10 billion.)

Other costs that have been mentioned in connection with the Vietnam War are less direct and more unmanageable in terms of estimation. For example it is claimed that there could have been a reduction in the nation's productive capacity due to the shifting of resources from the private to the defense sector. If true, this would represent a cost to future generations who would not receive the capacity to produce and consume the volume of goods they would have in the absence of the diversion of resources.[21]

Similarly, the defense establishment itself was forced to cut back on weapons research, development, testing, and construction. These cutbacks would create a backlog that would have to be made up after the war was concluded. However they really represent a cost of the war and should be included as such. The Cornell University Air War Group estimated the deferred costs at $15 billion.[22]

Furthermore the war induced many other indirect effects, some of them more pertinent in the short run and others over longer time periods. Inflation causes many redistributions among income groups, but who wins and loses in the game is not always clear. Similarly war-induced monetary and fiscal policies affect the level of output and employment as well as what is produced and who is employed as a result. Here value judgments enter into the analysis; if inflation or government policies affect the distributions of income and wealth adversely, i.e., make them more inequitable, is that a cost of the war or the natural outcome of the economic system with its distribution of rewards and penalties? Could or would these adverse effects be reversed once the war-related conditions have passed?

One analyst, Robert Stevens, attributed the recession of 1970–72 to the war-induced government policies and added $185 billion to the war bill. In his view the overheated war economy was cooled by a recession, a recession that would not have occurred had there been no war. The measure of the cost to the economy is the potential GNP that it might have enjoyed minus the actual GNP that was realized. For the years 1970–73, the GNP sacrificed was about $185 billion.[23] This procedure assumes that the economy would have operated at its potential throughout the period and was prevented from doing so because of the war. This is certainly a possibility, but it is a rather strong assumption to make considering how few times the economy has performed up to its potential.

He also included as a cost of the war the excess inflation from 1965–72 of $140 billion. Taking 2 percent inflation as the target rate of inflation, he multiplied the actual inflation rate in excess of 2 percent in each year by the GNP to arrive at an estimate of the cost of excess inflation. Painful as the inflation might have been, it is not realistic to measure costs in this manner nor is it even a cost since many benefited from rising prices. More likely income was redistributed in this period but that is not the same thing as a cost to the nation.[24]

Finally, he estimated $8 billion as a cost stemming from the loss of international trade due to the deteriorating terms of trade caused by inflation. The loss stems from the two devaluations of the dollar in terms of gold: one in 1971, and the other in 1973. The devaluation of the dollar added about 10 percent to the average cost of imports. Using 1972 as an example, Stevens estimated the cost of imports in that year to be about $8 billion.[25]

These indirect costs total $378 billion, hardly a trifling amount. These costs are more debatable than direct costs, and many would disagree with them, both in theory and in their estimation.

Additional costs could easily be pursued. Housing starts were reduced due to high interest rates; education could have been underfunded, hurting future generations; urban problems could have been ignored; drug problems were allowed to develop and become widespread; the Great Society programs in general were allowed to languish and many pressing social problems simply were not met; and so on. With a little imagination it would be easy to impute many more costs to the Vietnam War but they become more tenuous the greater the imagination.

Unfortunately, there is no calculus that would allow us to determine these costs in the absence of the war. What might have been cannot be ascertained. Moreover some of these costs could have been reversed following the war and were thus temporary disturbances to the economy. Quite simply, no real methodology exists that permits us to estimate the indirect costs involved nor how much of them can be attributed to the Vietnam War.[26] It is quite possible, however, that the total indirect costs involved could be in the hundreds of billions range.

BENEFITS

Our primary concern has been over the costs of the war and that is proper but are there no benefits to counterbalance the costs? Surely some benefits from the defense buildup and war-related economic activity are conceivable.

Individual members of the armed forces may benefit in a variety of ways. Some receive training that will enable them to secure a better civilian job when they leave the service. These benefits could be substantial but again there is the difficulty in estimating them. Sjaastad cites an unpublished study done by Phillips Cutright of the Social Security Administration that tabulated a large sample of the effects of military service on the subsequent earnings of selected individuals. The results indicate "no net positive effect of the military service on future earnings except possibly for persons in the lowest mental groups."[27] Cutright concluded the positive benefits of this group did not outweigh the negative effects of others who were removed from the civilian labor force. (In the next chapter, we will return to the experience of the Vietnam veteran when he returned to civilian life.)

Other veterans will be able to take advantage of the veterans' benefits and receive additional education, receive subsidized housing, etc. However, these have already been accounted for as *costs* and cannot be counted again as benefits. Simply put, the society would not have had to incur these costs had not the war occurred.

There could be spillover benefits to the civilian economy from technological advances in the military sector. It is possible that research for military purposes could lead to new inventions, techniques, or materials that might be useful in the production of civilian goods. Examples of past spillovers include computer technology, commercial airjets, and nuclear energy. However it is argued by many that the diversion of research and development into primarily military applications has robbed the private sector with the result that domestic industries declined. In nations where there is little diversion of R & D expenditures into military hardware, such as Japan and West Germany, consumer products and industries have flourished, and they have out-competed the United States.[28] So the spillover effects of defense spending are controversial even if they could be identified and measured.

There is also the traditional argument, attributed mainly to Marxists but others have joined in from time to time, that military expenditures are needed to keep the economy booming. Increased expenditures on defense stimulate the economic system; output and employment expand, and the economy booms. In the absence of such stimulation, the economy would stagnate. This argument has some merit, and several instances of defense buildups leading to a booming economy can be found in U.S. history. World War II took us out of the depression, and the Korean War followed by the cold war kept the economy growing. But what of the Vietnam War?

The rapid defense buildup under Kennedy, to close the nonexistent missile gap, helped to get the economy moving again towards the New Frontier. Along with the tax cuts of 1964, the economy was growing out of stagnation and reaching toward full employment when the Vietnam War began in earnest. Thus while military spending helped to create the growing economy, the Vietnam War was not "needed" to stimulate the economic system. In fact it overstimulated it, and "overfull" employment and inflation ensued.

Another contention of many is that adventures of this kind are undertaken to exploit the natural resources of a less developed country (LDC) or to take advantage of unequal trade relations in order to dump goods on the LDC, or interfere in other ways with its economic development and independence. However valid such an argument in other parts of the world, the situation in Vietnam does not fit the picture. There really are no natural resources to speak of, and even the oil discovered late in the war did not provoke much interest. Neither did trade considerations prompt the intervention into Indochina. U.S. firms were not eagerly waiting to invest in South Vietnam to exploit local economic conditions. In brief, the usual charges against foreign interventions did not hold in this instance.

Rabid anticommunism can always be suggested as a cause for concern in any part of the world. Reflexive reactions to any uprising that even suggests any form of collectivism can be expected to follow from those like Johnson and Nixon who were sensitive to charges of "losing" another country to communism. Perhaps the reactions were more subtle and represent a new form of imperialism. In the words of Melman,

> The methods of the new imperialism included direct wielding of military, political and economic power to checkmate leftist nationalism and to take direct political control of entire nations— without relying on, and even in the absence of, economic mechanisms of trade and investment that were basic to the older imperialism.[29]

Given the foreign policies of the Reagan administration in the Caribbean and Central America, this explanation cannot be dismissed. But the enormous costs that were incurred in order to make this policy operational and to give it credence represent a tragic waste of resources and human life.

OTHER DOMESTIC BENEFITS

We know that the growth of real wages did not increase in the period but actually declined after 1965 and turned negative in 1970. Similarly corporate profits did not increase as was seen in Chapter 4. Again it would be necessary to follow the paths of income and wealth redistributions to determine who won and lost in this period of inflation and full employment. The overall distributions of wealth are not available for comparisons, but the distribution of income shows little change over the period in question with a small improvement in the lower ends of the distribution in 1966 when the lowest fifth of the population increased its share of aggregate income to 5.6 percent from 5.2 percent in 1965, and the second fifth increased its share in the same period to 12.4 percent from 12.2 percent. Thereafter they stabilized once again. The increases came at the expense of the highest fifth of the population. There is nothing dramatic here although the data are highly aggregated and may not show all the movements that occurred.

It would hardly be surprising to discover that defense contractors would be beneficiaries of war-related expenditures. However the data would not always reveal the extent of profits because contractors may not be able to separate commercial from defense work, are not required to report profits on contracts, and because their profits are stated as a percent of costs and not on a return of investment basis. If all the costs are not accounted for when government property is used by contractors, a flat percentage rate of profit would be misleading, and a rate of return on investment would be more accurate. A $1 million dollar contract with a 10 percent rate of return would yield a profit of $100,000; if however, the contractor had to utilize only $500,000 of its equipment, then the rate of return on its investment would be 20 percent.

SUMMARY AND CONCLUSIONS

To review the total costs and benefits involved in the Vietnam War experience, Table 6.4 summarizes the costs accounted for in earlier discussions.[30]

According to Table 6.4, the total costs incurred in the Vietnam War were over $500 billion and could range up to $900 billion if other costs are included. These are staggering sums for "a war that nobody won—a struggle between victims. Its origins were complex, and its legacy remains to be assessed by future generations. But whether a valid venture or misguided endeavor, it was a tragedy of epic dimensions."[31]

Table 6.4
Summary of Costs of Vietnam War (in Billions of Dollars)

Direct Budgetary Costs (Table 6.1)	$ 173
Future Budgetary Costs (Table 6.2)	251
Economic Costs of the War (Table 6.3)	83
Foreign Trade Costs	8
Total Costs of the Vietnam War	$ 515

Note: If the costs calculated by others ($378 billion for recessions and inflation, the deterioration in trade conditions, and the $15 billion for deferred military investment) is added to the above sum, the total would rise to $900 billion.

It takes little imagination to wonder what sums like these could have accomplished if used for other purposes. The Great Society was sacrificed, urban problems were allowed to fester and grow, mass transportation was discarded, schools were ignored, and so on. There is little point in belaboring the issue or in listing the social ills—the butter, that was sacrificed for guns. Whether or not these problems would have been addressed in the absence of the war is problematical anyway, and little is gained in speculation. It is sufficient to point to the enormous waste of resources in the pursuit of unspecified goals and thereby hope to avoid its repetition.

The enormity of the folly is evident when one looks at the benefits of the war. That no one, except perhaps for defense contractors, seems to have benefited appears distressing in view of the costs involved. True, as in most cost-benefit analyses, the costs may be easier to measure than the benefits, but more gains should be readily identifiable. Only the military sector appears to show temporary gains, either for contractors or in promotions for officers who reported for battle. The rest of society was badly divided with little in economic gains to smooth over the dissention.

Considering the total costs minus the total benefits leaves only one conclusion—it was not a worthwhile endeavor. Looking at costs and benefits are one way to pass judgment but whether considered from an economic, legal, moral, or military view, the same conclusion emerges— the war cannot be justified.

NOTES

1. Robert W. Stevens, *Vain Hopes, Grim Realities* (New York: New Viewpoints, 1976), 93.

2. Thomas C. Thayer, "The American Style to War Made it Costly," in *The Lessons of Vietnam* edited by W. Scott Thomson and Donaldson D. Frizzell (New York: Crane, Russak, 1977), 209–10. The same points are made by Senator Vance Hartke in his early book on the war, *The American Crisis in Vietnam* (New York: Bobbs-Merrill, 1968), 100–115.

3. Ibid., 96. Stevens estimated that 38,000 military personnel were on hand at the end of 1964. The support cost (at a rate of two support personnel per one directly involved is then $836 million per year (38,000 x 2 x $11,000 per person). For the nine years, the total comes to $7.5 billion. The remaining $7.5 billion results from official estimates made after the official reports began to issue both full and incremental costs. Stevens maintains that the estimate understated full costs in fiscal year 1967 by $4.4 billion. For fiscal years 1965 and 1966 no full costs were reported at all, and Stevens estimated the adjustment needed for these years at $3 billion.

4. United States Senate, Committee on Foreign Relations, Subcommittee on United States *Security Agreements and Commitments Abroad, part 6, Republic of Korea*, 91st Congress, second session, February 1970, 1552. In the course of these hearings, Senator

Fulbright raised many questions of U.S. policy in Southeast Asia and particularly in regard to the enticing of other nations to join the United States in a war to which he was opposed.

5. Lieutenant General Stanley R. Larsen and Brigadier General James L. Collins, Jr., *Allied Participation in Vietnam* (Washington, D.C.: Department of the Army, 1975), 160–69. The actual troop strength is given in Table 6.5, from page 23 of their book.

Table 6.5
Military Assistance Forces, 1964–70

Country	1964	1965	1966	1967	1968	1969	1970
Australia	200	1557	4525	6818	7661	7672	6763
Korea	200	20620	45566	47829	50003	48869	48537
Thailand	–	16	244	2205	6005	11568	11586
New Zealand	30	119	155	534	516	552	441
Philippines	17	72	2061	2020	1576	189	74

6. See the Committee of Concerned Asian Scholars, *The Indochina Story* (New York:Bantam Books, 1970), 138–44.

7. See the prepared statement of James L. Clayton in U.S. Congress, Joint Economic Committee, Subcommittee on Economy in Government, *The Military Budget and National Economic Priorities*, 91st Congress, 1st session, part 1, June 1969, 146.

8. James L. Clayton, "The Fiscal Cost of the Cold War to the United States: The First 25 Years, 1947–1971," in *The Western Political Quarterly* 66 (September 1972): 375–95. The table appears on page 387.

9. John M. Clark, *The Costs of the World War to the American Public* (New Haven: Yale University Press, 1931), 203.

10. Clayton, JEC Hearings, *The Military Budget and National Economic Priorities*, 148.

11. Robert Eisner, "The War and the Economy," in *Why Are We Still in Vietnam?* edited by Sam Brown and Len Ackland (New York: Random House, 1970), 119.

12. *The Report of the President's Commission on an All-Voluntary Armed Force* (Washington, D.C.: U.S. Government Printing Office, February 1970), Chapter 3, 23–33.

13. Robert Eisner, "The War and the Economy," 119. The estimation procedure employed is given in the Appendix, 122–23.

14. Cornell University Air War Study Group, *The Air War in Indochina*, rev. ed. (Boston: Beacon Press, 1972), 106 and 240. The equations of the two studies are:

$$\text{Cornell: ACC} = (-26.21) + (38.32)\,(\text{AF}) - (18.00)\,(\text{AF})^2 + (2.88)\,(\text{AF})^3$$

$$\text{Eisner's ACC} = (-52.93) + (71.12)\,(\text{AF}) - (31.24)\,(\text{AF})^2 + (4.64)\,(\text{AF})^3$$

Where ACC stands for Added Costs of Conscription in billions of dollars, and AF is total military personnel in millions. The estimates differ because of updated data used in the later Cornell study.

15. Stevens, *Vain Hopes, Grim Realities*, 184. Stevens took the difference between the average yearly wage of a beginning unskilled blue-collar worker, $5,400, and the military base pay, $1,655, and multiplied the difference, $3,745 times the estimated many years spent by servicemen in Vietnam, 3,873,975 to arrive at his estimate of sacrificed earnings of $14.6 billion.

16. See the statement of Robert Eisner in Congress of the United States, Joint Economic Committee, Subcommittee on Economy in Government, *Changing National Priorities*, 91st Congress, second session, part 2, June 1970, 677–78. In this statement, Eisner used a 2 percent growth rate for earnings and discounted the total by a discount rate of 5 percent to yield a present value of $11.6 billion. He also calculated the costs of disability and hospitalization at $11.5 billion. In this book only current values are used because it would be difficult to compare some values on a current basis and others on a present value basis; also the focus here is on total cost dollars and not the total costs at a particular time.

17. For those who are interested, the *present value* of the earnings loss using a productivity rate increase of 2 percent and a discount rate of 5 percent and an initial income loss of $10,000 is $13.5 billion. The casualties in the war amounted to 153,000. With the assumption that the mean disability rate is 33 percent the *present value* of the earnings loss due to disability or hospitalization is $11.9 billion. The total future earnings loss discounted to 1970 is $25.4 = ($13.5 + $11.9) which is not very different from the $23 billion used in the text.

18. Leonard Dudley and Peter Passell, "The War in Vietnam and the United States Balance of Payments," *The Review of Economics and Statistics* (November 1971): 437–42.

19. For a contrary view of the balance of payments problem see, Department of Defense, Comptroller, *The Economics of Defense Spending: A Look at the Realities*, July 1972, 67–71. While admitting that defense expenditures contributed to the decline in the balance of payments in the 1950s, they no longer did so in the later years of the 1970s. The data presented to support this contention are not suitable for analysis for the Vietnam period since only selected years are supplied, and the most important years of the war, 1965–67 are missing.

20. Stevens, *Vain Hopes, Grim Realities*, 109.

21. Cornell University Air War Study Group, *Air War*, 105.

22. Ibid., 104.

23. Stevens, *Vain Hopes, Grim Realities*, 158.

24. Ibid., 161.

25. Ibid., 110.

26. For more discussion of these concerns and some attempt at formulating a methodology see Bruce M. Russett, "The Price of War," in *The War Economy of The United States* edited by Seymour Melman (New York: St. Martin's Press, 1971), 152–60; Jerry Hollenhorst and Gary Ault, "An Alternative Answer to: Who Pays for Defense?," *American Political Science Review* 65 (September 1971): 760–63; See also J. S. Grant,

A. G. Moss, and J. Unger, *Cambodia: The Widening War in Indochina: A Primer* (New York: Washington Square Press, 1971).

27. Larry A. Sjaastad, "The Conscription Tax" in *The President's Commission on an All-Volunteer Armed Force*, Part IV, 1–11.

28. For example see Seymour Melman, "Who Decides Technology?, in *The War Economy of the United States*, edited by Seymour Melman, 149. Among many others see, Robert B. Reich, *The Next American Frontier* (New York: Times Books, 1983), 190–93.

29. Seymour Melman, *The Permanent War Economy* (New York: Simon and Schuster, 1974), 266.

30. It is important to note that all the data are given in current dollars—just actual amounts without regard to time. This is clearly inappropriate for costs that extend well into the future. Such costs should be discounted to the present so that they can be properly viewed and compared with the costs as of now. (The costs should be reduced to their present value; failure to do so would deny that a rate of interest exists.) While technically correct in regard to future costs, there are several problems with present values in this situation. First, the Department of Defense and many others quoted in this book, use absolute dollars to describe costs, and it would be misleading to compare their data. Second, what discount rate to use would be arbitrary, especially when the costs are spread out over many years. Third, even if a proper rate of discount could be agreed upon, our concern is not with the costs of the war at a certain date, but with total estimated costs. Present values in this case would be misleading rather than enlightening. Fourth, we are not interested in how the costs will be repaid, or in future budgetary problems. Inter-generational shifts of resources are not our immediate concern.

31. Stanley Karnow, *Vietnam* (New York: Viking Press, 1983), 11.

7   THE POST-VIETNAM SOCIETY

When the U.S. involvement in the war ended in January 1973, attention shifted to the release of American prisoners of war. In February the first group of them landed on Clark Field in the Philippines. Gradually more of them were freed and by April, all of them were. With their release, U.S. interest in Vietnam seemed to wane, and the ongoing war seemed even farther away than it did when U.S. troops were fighting.

The war, of course, was turned over to the South Vietnamese who were at first highly spirited, but gradually the deteriorating economy, the lack of training and materiel, the absence of U.S. support, the official corruption, the lack of leadership, and so on, were too much for their armed forces, and the war was quickly lost. On April 30, 1975 the North Vietnamese captured Saigon and accepted the surrender of the South Vietnamese forces. Earlier in April, Cambodia fell to the Khmer Rouge, and another period of repression and turmoil began in Southeast Asia.

Thus the war drifted on, and the upheaval spread into neighboring Cambodia; but even as the fighting became more fierce and brutal, as refugees wandered in search of a stable area, and as the savagery toward rival groups, civilians, refugees, and prisoners became unspeakable, the war faded into the background of American consciousness. The nation turned its back on a long and painful adventure and was anxious to forget the whole thing and relegate it to historians. To some, the United States lost a war against a far inferior enemy; the cause was noble but the United States abandoned its principles and surrendered to popular sentiment. Yet to others, the cause was ignoble and unworthy of a great nation; to these people, the U.S. involvement was wrong to begin with and losing or winning was irrelevant. There were, as usual, all shades of opinion in between and all shades of bewilderment over the whole affair. In short, the war's conclusion left no one happy with either the outcome or the aftermath. Relief over the war's end was mixed with bitterness and sorrow, and for many, shame, either because we entered into it or because we failed to win it.

On the domestic scene, Richard Nixon facing impeachment had resigned on August 9, 1974, and was replaced by Vice President Gerald Ford who had replaced Spiro Agnew who was forced out as Nixon's vice president. President Ford, in a very controversial action, promptly pardoned Nixon for all federal crimes he "committed or may have committed." This rapid and unprecedented turnover at the top of government was accomplished with a minimum of disorder, attesting more to the stability of U.S. political institutions than to the lack of moral indignation.

STAGFLATION

So mid-1974 was not a happy time for the country, and it was not a very propitious time for Ford to become president. The economy was sliding into another recession, but that would not be recognized until late in the year. With the removal of price controls, inflation could no longer be suppressed and prices "bulged" as everyone scrambled to restore past relations. Inflation quickly became the number one concern of the administration, and Ford set about trying to combat it by proposing a tax increase and a "whip inflation now" (WIN) program, complete with button, whose aims were as questionable as the button was ludicrous. Inflation was indeed a problem but the policies used to combat it did not recognize the causes. A series of events led to the growth of inflation, and they became cumulative. The dollar was devalued in 1973 causing import prices to rise; food prices rose following crop failures in 1972–74; energy prices, especially oil prices, increased as the oil producing countries demanded higher prices; and price controls were removed sending everyone scrambling to recover lost market positions.[1] These essentially one-time price increases were allowed to become part of the core inflation and became cumulative.

Thus, for instance, when the price of oil rose following the OPEC embargo on shipments to the United States sending the CPI to double digits in 1974, aggregate demand was reduced. Interest rates rose with a tight monetary policy to their highest rates in modern times, crushing the housing market. The prime rate rose to nearly 12 percent, mortgage rates to over 10 percent, and the Federal Reserve's discount rate increased to 8 percent. Preoccupied with inflation, the Ford administration proposed a tax increase and restricted the growth of government expenditures. As a result inventories piled up, production and output fell drastically, and unemployment rose steadily, reaching 8.8 percent in the second quarter of 1975. In short the economy entered into the sharpest recession since the 1930s. It was a brief but sharp recession lasting from November 1973 to March 1975. Real GNP fell by 6.6 percent over the decline, but prices continued to rise as the CPI increased by 14.7 percent in the downturn. Of course, capacity usage declined, and the utilization rate of our productive capacity fell to 68 percent from 83 percent. Stagflation, high unemployment combined with inflation, was painfully evident in this period. Again tight money and fiscal restraint were employed to fight inflation and instead brought on this sharp recession.

The economy recovered as the private sector led the way, but monetary policy was erratic, and fiscal policy was expansionary thanks to the tax cuts of 1975 taking effect. Again treating price shocks to the system by the usual monetary and fiscal policies made things even worse and contributed to the recession that followed.

The administration did reverse itself, proposed a tax decrease, and did try to reduce government spending. The problem is that monetary and fiscal policies are not effective in fighting stagflation. The oil embargo was lifted, and the economy did recover somewhat but was still stagnating in 1976. Ford lost the election of 1976 to Carter, but the economic problems remained regardless of who was in the White House.

More price shocks hit the Carter administration with much the same effect. Again food prices and oil prices rose, interest rates increased, and the revolution in Iran cut off oil supplies from that nation. Inflation accelerated as the CPI rose from 6.8 percent in 1977, to 13.3 percent in 1979, and 12.4 percent in 1980. Meanwhile, unemployment remained around 7 percent, falling slightly in 1978 and 1979 but returning to 7.1 percent in 1980. President Carter even resurrected a form of wage guideposts in the effort to slow inflation. He resorted to voluntary wage guidelines as the Kennedy administration had done in 1962. The program called for labor to limit its demands to 7 percent (later increased to a range from 7.5 to 9.5 percent, hoping for a average wage settlement of 8.5 percent) and for firms to limit their price increases to 0.5 percent below past average increases. This time the policy was much less successful. Real wages fell in the 1970s, and it was not the time to ask labor to make sacrifices in the national interest. Later he asked for and received some credit controls[2] that might have worked for a while to curb consumer spending, but the effects were short-lived and ended up merely irritating everyone opposed to government regulations of the economy.

The Carter administration thus found itself in the same bind that confined the Ford administration. It took office wanting to pursue policies that would encourage growth, advocating tax decreases and expenditure increases. Monetary policy had been expected to be accommodating as well. But energy and food price increases put an end to unequivocal macroeconomic policies. The administration became cautious, and monetary policy became erratic in the face of inflation and the changing monetary conditions outlined earlier. More tax reductions were sought to combat stagflation but inflation made some sort of controls appear necessary. The voluntary controls were meant to signal the administration's concern for inflation while it attempted to pump up the economy.

In 1979 the second wave of severe energy price shocks forced a reversal of economic policies. Government expenditures were restrained, and monetary policy became very tight. In October 1979, the Federal Reserve turned to monetarists' policies and concentrated on restricting the growth of the money supply and let interest rates react to market conditions. Interest rates surpassed all earlier ones and recession threatened. Again the administration fought inflation with tight money and tight budgets. The result was another recession in 1980 with consumer prices increasing by double digits and with interest rates approaching 20 percent. The unemployment rate stood at over 7 percent.

In summary, lacking any alternatives to traditional fiscal and monetary policies, the administration turned to fighting stagflation with methods that did not confront the problems causing great discontent among the electorate. In 1980 the voters showed their displeasure as they turned to different solutions to their perceived economic problems.

SUMMARY OF POLICY RESPONSES

As we have seen, price shocks and energy problems in general plagued both the Ford and Carter administrations. The tendencies toward stagnation were evident throughout the 1970s, and the attempts to solve the problems through traditional monetary and fiscal policies were ineffective. Tax cuts did relieve some of the political pressure caused by higher taxes on inflated incomes. Inflation pushed people into higher tax brackets, and this "bracket creep" caused much consternation among taxpayers who were forced to pay higher taxes on inflated money incomes without feeling better off. Cutting taxes acted as an escape valve for taxpayer discontent;

the tax reductions were a crude way of adjusting the tax code for inflation (indexing it), something which the Congress was unwilling to do as a matter of policy.

Tight monetary policies did not work either, as the stop-and-go policies of the Federal Reserve System gave off conflicting signals and helped cause recessions in order to fight inflation. In the end, the higher food and energy prices found their way into higher wage demands and into further inflation—the price shocks were allowed to become part of the core inflation. At the same time, labor costs mounted as the rate of growth of labor productivity began to decline, slowly at first and then dramatically in 1973. In the 1970s, the problem of stagflation seemed intractable.

But a review of the macroeconomic policies of the 1970s, however brief, is not the purpose of this section, and that analysis can readily be found in other sources.Thus without a thorough examination, I will assume that the major problem in the immediate post–Vietnam War period was stagflation caused in part by one-time events, such as food and energy price shocks and by reactions in the post-price control period. The question then becomes: What has this to do with the Vietnam War?

INFLATION AND WAGE AND PRICE CONTROLS

Earlier it was suggested that the wage and price control system of the Nixon administration was mainly politically inspired, and its real economic content was directed at international trade conditions. That assertion remains unchanged, but it is necessary to understand that the controls were greeted with relief—stemming from the belief that something was being done about inflation at last. Many were growing weary of continued price increases and welcomed the attempt to control them. Firms wanted to restrain the demands of labor, while labor and consumers wanted to control price increases. Those price increases were the result of the Vietnam war buildup that produced excess demand inflation and later supply side inflation. Thus had there been no inflation, there would not have been the excuse for wage and price controls. The rise in prices allowed the administration to impose controls to accomplish its purposes—reelection—as well as deal with the international problems that required a crisis atmosphere to resolve.

The inflation caused by the war can thus be held responsible for a whole string of actions starting with controls, flexible exchange rates rather than the fixed rates, removal of gold from trade settlements, devaluations of the dollar, and so on. However, it is not wise to extend the list into areas that are too far removed from the actual events of the war, and it is always difficult to separate those actions that would have taken place anyway from those that were war-induced. For example, as part of the controls system, protectionist measures (repeal of the excise taxes) for the auto and trucking industries were inserted, but these might have been in process before, and the controls merely offered a convenient vehicle to accomplish the policy in the shadow of more dramatic actions.

INFLATION AND OIL PRICES

Similarly, the increases in the price of oil of 1973–74 and 1979–80 were largely the result of inflation in the Western nations, particularly the United States. Oil revenues of the OPEC countries are used for economic development and represent for some nations the main avenue for economic and social progress. These nations import a wide array of goods from other, more developed, countries. The imports include not only the capital goods necessary for development but manufactured goods of all kinds, as well as raw materials and foodstuffs. Yet these oil-producing nations watched as inflation eroded the purchasing power of their oil revenues. To make matters even worse for the oil producing countries, the oil contracts were denominated in dollars. With inflation in the United States, the dollar was depreciating against Western European currencies, and thus the oil producing countries were hit twice. If they purchased goods from the United States, their dollars did not buy as much due to inflation in the United States; if they bought goods from Western Europe, their dollars also did not buy as much due to the depreciating dollar.

Moreover, from 1950 to 1970, the price of oil was either stable or falling while the prices of imports continued to rise; from 1965 on the increase in import prices accelerated and the real incomes of the oil producers fell more rapidly.[3]

Thus the oil producing countries attempted to recover the loss of real income by raising prices, but these price increases were forced on the economies already staggering from recessions and tending toward stagnation. In the words of my colleague Abbas Alnasrawi:

The OPEC oil-price increases of 1973–74 and 1979–80 represented serious shocks to the economies of the industrialized countries. These external shocks were superimposed on economies that had already entered a period of slow growth or of no growth or that were already experiencing a serious decline in output. These changes in output were also associated with high rates of unemployment and persistent inflation, giving rise to conditions of stagflation.[4]

It is certainly true that the Arab members of OPEC did use oil as a foreign policy weapon when they imposed an oil embargo to punish the United States for its support of Israel in the Arab-Israeli conflict of 1973. The fall in purchasing power of oil revenues was clearly not the only impetus for the push for higher oil prices. Still without the inflation in industrialized countries, there would have been less pressure to increase oil revenues to support economic development. The common enemy, Israel, served to make their oil policies more acceptable to the participating Arab states and gave their plans more cohesion and unity than might otherwise have been the case; but the embargo was meant more to send a message to the United States to exert pressure on Israel than to threaten the United States directly. Oil price increases alone would not have sent this message. The price increases have to be separated from the foreign policy aspects since they were sincere attempts to recover some of the lost real income caused by the rising prices of imports, and the rising prices of imports can be largely traced, at least since 1965, to the overheated economy caused by the Vietnam War.

The consequences of the energy problems of the 1970s are many. Autos were redesigned, homes were better insulated, appliances were made more energy efficient, nuclear power became more acceptable, coal was used more causing air pollution problems, conservation of energy sources began in earnest, population shifts from the North to the Sunbelt occurred, and the manufacturing process turned more to energy-saving, labor-using technology. Too many adjustments were made in the economy to tabulate, and while not all of them can be traced to the oil problems of the 1970s, there is no question that many of them were initiated as a result of oil price increases, and the embargo, and the threats of their recurrence. To some extent, these reactions can be attributed to the inflation of the late 1960s and early 1970s, although a precise accounting is impossible.

INFLATION, HOUSING, AND SAVING

Once the origins of inflation are identified (and it is assumed that the Vietnam War is one of them), it is tempting to trace the repercussions on other markets that are seemingly unrelated to the immediate causes. The economic system is a giant labyrinth and events in one area interact with those in another to cause reactions of a third kind. Inflation is a good example of the type of disturbance that can set off chain reactions of various kinds in disparate areas. It would be interesting for example to see some of the effects on the housing market and on household saving. Attributing all the reactions to the inflation induced by the Vietnam War would be stretching things, of course, but some of the repercussions in these markets can be traced back to that original source of the inflation and its effects in the 1970s.

A large part of the housing boom in the 1970s can be attributed to inflation and the housing subsidy supplied by the tax code. In the 1970s, inflation averaged 7.4 percent and mortgage interest rates 8.8 percent. For someone in the 40 percent tax bracket this meant that the mortgage interest rate was really 5.3 percent (60 percent of 8.8 percent) since mortgage interest is deductible for tax purposes. However since inflation was rising at 7.4 percent, the real mortgage rate was -1.9 percent. This represents a nice subsidy for home buyers, but that is not the primary issue here.[5] It is inflation that reduces the cost of home ownership and induces more investment into housing than into other types of investment. While the investment in housing may not have been all that bad, the decision to invest more in this sector should have been made on other than tax considerations. Particularly since low-income, public housing did not benefit from these subsidies, and that is where the need for housing probably was the greatest.

Since housing competes for saving with all other types of investment, the more resources devoted to housing, the less will be available for other investment. Thus inflation and the tax code steer investment into certain channels and away from others. Moreover the saving rate in the United States has never been very high and has actually been falling in the 1980s.[6] The competition for the limited funds may adversely affect business investment and limit economic growth. Together with the huge federal deficits in the 1980s, the savings consumed by the housing market had diminished the funds available to increase the capital stock of the nation.[7]

Investment in housing is also encouraged by the expectations of continued inflation that assumes housing prices would continue to rise as well. In fact if housing prices rise faster than the rate of inflation, the homeowner benefits again with capital gains that are not taxed and when they are taxed have special provisions attached to them. Indeed inflationary expectations may well encourage consumption at the expense of saving. The huge increase in personal debt may well be attesting to this condition as well as to the reduction in the saving rate.

This is not the place to pursue these issues since they take us farther away from the main topic. These points are made to suggest the many ramifications of inflation as it makes its way through the economic system. So when an inflationary period begins, it is not sufficient to identify only the immediate effects on the economy but one must look to longer run consequences as well. Thus, long after the Vietnam War can be blamed for the immediate inflation, it can still be blamed for instituting the inflation and its subsequent reactions. Long after the pebble thrown into a pool has sunk to the bottom and out of sight, the ripples continue.

OTHER ECONOMIC DEVELOPMENTS

It would be interesting to see how a few of the structural changes suggested in Chapter 4 affected the economy in the 1970s. The stagnation of the 1970s, already discussed, can be seen in some of the elements of the structural change.

The productivity of labor continued to decline from past growth rates. Output per hour of all persons, one measure of productivity, declined dramatically in 1973 to a growth rate of 1.8 percent and the rate of growth actually turned negative in 1974 to -2.2 percent and did not recover to the previous rate for the remainder of the decade. The rate of growth of labor productivity did not begin to return to historical averages until 1983, and then it fell off again. There was no unique explanation for the decline then, and even now, too many explanations have been offered to be credible to everyone.

The utilization of our productive capacity also continued to decline in the 1970s. For the decade, the average usage of capacity for all industries was 82 percent but the rate for manufacturing was only 80 percent. No great change can be found in the 1980s with the all-industry and manufacturing categories both averaging around 81 percent. More disturbing perhaps is the rate for durable goods manufacturing which remained at 78 percent, far below the rates of the 1960s. In the latter half of the decade, however, all capacity utilization rates were slowly increasing. Much discussion in recent years over the decline of manufacturing and the rise of the service sector in the United States has followed the analysis of data like these.[8] If these and other data are indicative of a real shift in the product mix of U.S. output, it would represent a profound structural change of the U.S. economy, a change that may have begun in the 1960s.

The fall in the rate of growth of corporate profits appears to have been arrested. The observed decline in the late 1960s and early 1970s was reversed later in the decade. However, the 1980s again showed a decline in the rate of growth of corporate profits. Evidently there is more to this complex variable than can be discussed here. Measurement problems abound, but even if these could be overcome, much more study is required before much can be determined about the extent of structural change and corporate profits.

In the social area, the 1970s saw a retreat from the social programs of the 1960s. These were found to be too expensive, unworkable, self-defeating, unnecessary, and wasteful. In short, in the decade of inflation and stagnation, the American public became unwilling to finance social programs, and the experiments were largely abandoned. With real wages declining, interest rates soaring, and the prices of energy and food escalating, the public was in no mood to pay for programs they deemed undeserving. The war on poverty was reduced to skirmishes as the nation looked the other way.

One need only look at the tax revolt that started in California in 1978 to see the culmination of the years of frustration in paying taxes. The desire to limit taxes, in that case property taxes, was indicative of the feeling that taxes were "too high," and since property taxes furnished the revenue of localities to pay for education and welfare benefits, it is not too much to infer that some connection is plausible. Soon the idea of limiting taxes spread to other states and eventually to the nation in the Kemp-Roth federal income tax cut proposal in 1980. People were simply tired of paying taxes in general and for social programs in particular. When politicians told the public that such social programs were wasteful and unnecessary, and that the public was not getting its money's worth, it was easy to justify cutting them out by limiting revenues to pay for them.

When Ronald Reagan asked people if they were better off in 1980 than they were in 1976, many replied, "No." Their income gains, which they identified as well-earned, were eroded by inflation and rising taxes. Even if they were actually better off in real terms—their income gains exceeded inflation—they *felt* worse off. They felt they deserved the entire monetary income gains and felt cheated when inflation took some of the gains away. If someone's income increased by $1000 (which he or she regards as due to merit, conveniently forgetting that inflation boosts people's incomes as well) and rising prices take away $500 of the $1000, the person is still better off but feels cheated anyway for $1000 at the old prices would have meant a significant improvement in living standards.

Some of this feeling led to frustration over the lack of economic progress (each succeeding generation ought to have a higher living standard than the previous one) in the 1970s, and some is reflected in the swing toward more conservative ideas and away from experimentation. In economics this is seen by the succession of fiscally conservative leaders—Nixon, Ford, Carter, Reagan, and finally Bush. Fiscal policy continued to be found untrustworthy. The disenchantment with government and its ability to control the economy led many to reject the manipulation of the economy by altering taxes and expenditures. Monetary policy fared no better. The stop and go policy of the Federal Reserve, expansionary and then contractionary, produced many critics of discretionary actions.

Of course, it became evident to all, even if they would not admit it, that traditional monetary and fiscal policy could not fight stagflation. Still the traditional policies were pursued—there was nothing else to do now that policy experiments, such as another incomes policy, were ruled out. Inflation just continued as the economy was staggering. Since the government could not control the economy, it was one step away from concluding that maybe government was part (or all) of the problem.

Hence more calls for a balanced budget and more calls for a shift in monetary policy were heard. The pronouncements merely reflected the conservatives' desire for rules and the rejection of discretionary acts of bureaucrats. The balanced budget idea gained adherents, but was not enacted, although many states voted for a constitutional convention to consider one. The shift in monetary policy was accepted as the monetarists finally convinced the Fed to adopt its agenda. In October 1979, the Fed began to attempt to control the money supply instead of interest rates. The attempt lasted until 1982, when the Fed, in the face of the recession of 1980 and the recession of 1981–82, retreated from the experiment. Using mainly monetary policy to fight stagflation resulted in extremely high interest rates and helped bring on two recessions in a very short time. Monetarist influence remained after 1982 but gradually fell out of favor.

In 1980, the voters rejected whatever was left of Keynesian economics and elected Ronald Reagan, who promised a conservative revolution in policy-making. Liberalism, and liberal economic policies, not really in evidence in the 1970s, were rejected in favor of something new—supply side economics. In practice, this supply side economics that involved massive tax cuts to stimulate saving, investment, and GNP turned out to be more Keynesian than even Keynesian economists had advocated. The massive federal deficit that followed surely altered the economic agenda in the 1980s and may well have altered the economic structure in ways not fully realized at this time.

POST-VIETNAM MILITARY CHANGES

The image of the military was tarnished in the Vietnam War. Living up to the cliche that generals fight the last war in the latest one, the military establishment could not cope with the type of guerrilla warfare in Vietnam. Their forecasts for an early and complete victory by using men and materiel as they were used in World War II, or even Korea, brought the military establishment first approval, then disillusionment, then scorn, and finally ridicule.

Despite the large amount of resources employed in Southeast Asia, the armed forces accomplished very little. With no conquests of land, success was measured by macabre body counts that no one believed. With the use of defoliants, more disturbing questions were asked. All the reports of massacres, of drug use among the troops, of morale problems, and of heavy bombings and widespread destruction, did not endear very many to the conduct of the war.

So it is not surprising to find a postwar distrust in the military and military solutions. Many thought the war should have been fought until won; others were content to end it quickly and get out. Whatever the origin, there arose a caution about ever getting involved in such a conflict again. Politicians and generals alike came to recognize that this unpopular war had put a restraint on future military activities that no amount of discussions on diplomacy could accomplish. A modicum of humility (shame?) was allowed to penetrate the facade of invincibility. It was called the Vietnam syndrome.

Indeed, the intense opposition to the quagmire of Vietnam led to the enactment of the War Powers Act that severely restrained the president from engaging in military operations where U.S. lives might be endangered unless such actions were sanctioned by Congress. Presidential actions in the Vietnam War, such as Nixon's secret bombing of Cambodia, disturbed many in Congress and galvanized them into action. This, of course, was just one more manifestation of the conflict between the executive and legislative branches over who should control foreign policy. But clearly the irritation over the origin and conduct of the war convinced many in Congress that formal restrictions on future presidents were necessary.

The formal restraints of the law and informal constraints of the society placed on the executive branch were sufficient to deter military adventures for a decade after the war had ended. Both the Ford and Carter administrations felt the pressure, and while not free of disturbances in the world, managed to avoid the type of entanglements that Vietnam provided. The Ford administration was tested in the Mayaquez affair, when the U.S. merchant ship, Mayaquez, was seized by Cambodian forces in the Gulf of Siam and retrieved by U.S. forces, and when North Korea killed two American officers and wounded four others at the boundary line. The Carter administration had its problems in the Soviet invasion of Afghanistan and in the Middle East, Iran in particular. Yet none of these provocative situations resulted in the type of military action that would have required congressional approval. Both administrations felt the constraints and limited their responses.

When the Reagan administration took over, one of its principle foreign policy aims was to rid the nation of this Vietnam syndrome. Its large and rapid military buildup and its belligerent attitude toward the Soviet Union clearly signaled the desire for change in foreign affairs. A strong defense, it was felt, would not only deter communist aggression but would even reverse some previous gains, or at any rate, force concessions at the bargaining table. The Reagan Doctrine was born.

However to reverse the Vietnam syndrome and demonstrate the nation's resolve, more direct evidence was needed. The administration's intervention in Central America in general and in Nicaragua in particular provided the necessary opportunity. Its initial covert activities in Nicaragua followed by open involvement in supporting the U.S. backed and financed contras certainly demonstrated that the administration did not fear the type of engagement that could have led to another Vietnam and did not feel constrained by the Vietnam syndrome. All over Central America, the United States risked involvements that could have resulted in protracted entanglements. In Nicaragua, it found another quagmire, another military adventure not supported by the American public. But the Vietnam syndrome had been broken.

To emphasize the exorcism of the Vietnam nightmare, the administration embarked on a series of foreign policy moves that would prove to the world that the United States was ready to resume its role as an international policeman. The United States sent a peacekeeping force to Lebanon that actually took sides in the conflict; in 1983, the United States invaded Grenada with flimsy excuses to root out the socialist government; in 1986, the United States bombed Libya in order to retaliate for alleged terrorism against the United States; in 1987, the United States decided to protect shipping in the Persian Gulf against attacks from Iran or Iraq. In 1989, the United States invaded Panama to overthrow the dictator and alleged drug trafficker General Manuel Noreiga who had refused to recognize an election that put the opposition in power.

The pattern was clear: demonstrate America's resolve to intervene in trouble areas even if the United States was not directly affected. In addition to casting aside the Vietnam syndrome, another pattern was emerging. Note in the foregoing list that the United States has been increasingly involved in third world conflicts. It appears that the United States is altering its worldwide strategy. Now that the tensions between the United States and the Soviet Union have relaxed and nuclear treaties have been signed or are in the making, the evil empire of the early Reagan administration no longer poses the threat that was relied upon in order to furnish the excuse for the massive military buildup. The administration can now safely let its military alliances, such as NATO, be concerned with the old adversaries while the United States can concentrate on third world disruptions. The Pentagon's new doctrine has been labeled "low-intensity conflict" or (L.I.C.), and it is being applied to military adventures in third world countries. "As now conceived, L.I.C. as a doctrine has stretched to the point that it embraces almost any sort of short-term military activity that a President might seek to undertake—War Powers Act or no."[9]

The Reagan administration has thus succeeded in twisting the Vietnam syndrome to the extent that the public has generally supported its actions. Still the victory was not complete because the civil war in Nicaragua did not elicit public support, and remnants of the Vietnam syndrome remained.

THE RETURNING VETERAN

The society was forced to undergo other adjustments caused by the war. Many returning veterans of the war found a frigid welcome. An unpopular war generated little respect for those who fought it. But the guerilla war, with all its horrors, left many veterans with physical and mental problems which required special treatment. Physical problems were not new but more mental problems developed than were anticipated. Some of them surfaced long after the war's conclusion and became apparent in some bizarre behavior, often involving violence, sometimes to themselves, sometimes to others. Many veterans suffered from a set of symptoms that came to be known as "post-traumatic stress disorder." Its manifestations include guilt, depression, and paranoia, and these disorders often led to crime, suicide, and substance abuse.[10]

Drug addiction among veterans has caused problems not found in previous war veterans. Drugs were readily available in Southeast Asia, and those who had to endure the daily horrors of the war found solace in the escape offered by mind altering substances. Since many of the veterans were also black, poor, or from poor areas, their return only added to local drug problems that had emerged in the 1960s. Many other social problems ranging from child or wife abuse to alcoholism and crime could be traced to veterans unable to adjust to civilian life. These vets felt used by a thankless society, and their feelings of alienation emerged in various ways, some decidedly unsocial.

Where shall we find a calculus to measure these costs? Their omission from Chapter 6 is just another reminder that all the costs of this adventure can never be known, and perhaps the most devastating ones not even imagined.

Yet the returning veteran had to find a place in the society. Of course there were efforts to help him reenter civilian life. (They were mostly male, about 98 percent, as only 257,000 women were in the armed services during the Vietnam era, and of these, only 33,000 were involved in the Vietnam theater.) One of the earliest was Project Transition, designed to provide training or education or to help them find jobs. Priority was given to those who were disabled or who lacked transferable skills for the private sector. Most of the training was vocational in content, preparing veterans for post office work, and on the job training experience was provided by private industry. In terms of occupations, 29 percent were prepared for clerical and sales work, 22 percent in machine trades, 19 percent in structural work, 14 percent in managerial jobs, 6 percent in services and the remainder in farming, benchwork, and other skills.[11] Yet neither employers nor the veterans themselves thought the Veterans Administration (VA) did a very good job in training veterans or in finding them jobs.[12] Only 41 percent of employers gave the VA positive ratings, and only 8 percent of veterans rated the VA's job as excellent, and 33 percent as pretty good.

In addition, veterans had some reemployment rights with their previous employers providing certain conditions were met. If these conditions were met (minimum time in service, maintained qualifications for job) then the employer had to reinstate the veteran with appropriate status and pay as if he/she had never left the job. This program worked reasonably well with the VA resolving about 98 percent of the disputes without litigation.[13]

Moreover, local and state employment offices were instructed to give preferential assistance to veterans looking for a job. And while they were looking for work, veterans were entitled to unemployment compensation if they met state requirements. Thus there were programs in effect to aid the returning veteran, and if they did not always work to everyone's satisfaction, they were at least available.

Finally returning veterans were entitled, as veterans before them, to educational benefits. The GI Bill, passed in 1944, paid for the education and living expenses of veterans. Most of the veterans were using the benefit at the college level, but in the immediate years after the war, fewer veterans were taking advantage of the program than veterans of previous wars. One complaint of the Vietnam veterans was the delay in receiving funds while the educators felt that benefits were too low. Few thought that veterans were abusing the program.[14]

THE EMPLOYMENT EXPERIENCE

Veterans began entering the civilian labor force in 1969 when President Nixon began withdrawing troops from Southeast Asia. The withdrawals continued until 1975 when the last of the troops were evacuated. For the years 1969–71, the data show that the unemployment rate was higher for veterans than nonveterans. The younger veteran (20–24 years of age) had an even greater unemployment rate than the older veteran (25–29 years old). For example in the second quarter of 1971, the younger veteran had an unemployment rate of 12.4 percent compared to the older veteran's rate of 5.1 percent. The older veteran would, of course, be more experienced, possibly have more training, etc. For comparison, the nonveteran's unemployment rates for the same period and same age groups were 9.5 percent and 4.0 percent.[15]

These early data do provide evidence that the Vietnam veteran was having more difficulty finding employment than the nonveteran. The same is true throughout the period in question, 1969–71, and the higher rates do not depend upon the state of the economy. These data are for all veterans in the Vietnam war period regardless of whether they were in Southeast Asia or had served somewhere else. Perhaps it would be instructive to separate the Veterans into these two groups (Vietnam theater veterans and Vietnam-era veterans) and see if there are any significant differences between them, and between the experience 15 years or so after they began entering the labor force.

Two surveys of veterans were made by Sharon R. Cohany of the Bureau of Labor Statistics: one in April 1985, and one in November 1987.[16] Since the results are similar, the November 1987 data will be used in the following discussion. Briefly Cohany found that those who did not serve in Southeast Asia fared no worse than nonveterans in the labor market. The other group, the Vietnam theater veteran, and particularly the disabled of that group, were apparently at a disadvantage in the labor market.

Of the 7.9 million male veterans who served during the Vietnam War period, 93 percent are now between the ages of 30 and 54, with 67 percent being between the ages of 35–44. This is the age group of maximum participation in the labor force, and thus it is not surprising to find that 92 percent of Vietnam veterans are in the labor force. This high participation rate is very close to the rate of the nonveteran. However as soon as disability and service in Southeast Asia are considered, differences begin to appear.

Table 7.1 shows the employment status of Vietnam veterans by disability and location of service. About 10 percent (811,000) of those who served in the Vietnam era reported some degree of disability. Those with less severe disabilities (less than 30 percent rating) were participating in the labor force in much the same way as the nondisabled. As the degree of disability rises, the participation in the labor market falls until the most severely disabled leave the labor force altogether. This negative correlation is to be expected, as is the positive one relating unemployment with the severity of disability. The unemployment rate for the disabled was 6.2 percent compared to 4.7 percent for those without disability. For those with 60 percent disability, the veterans ascribed their difficulties to their physical condition; below 30 percent few attributed their employment problems to physical impairment.

The disabled, at least, were receiving compensation from the federal government depending on the degree of disability, and this fact must also be considered when looking at labor force participation rates. What of those who were not disabled? Some 300,000 veterans were looking for work in this period, or 4.7 percent of the total. The unemployment rate for nonveterans for the same period was 4.3 percent. For those who served in the Vietnam theater, the unemployment rate was 5.2 percent, while those who did not serve in Southeast Asia experienced a rate of 4.3 percent, the same rate as the nonveteran experienced.

Why the difference between those who served in the Vietnam theater and those who did not? Some of the difference can be explained by the educational attainment prior to entering the military. One study found that high school dropouts were one and one-half times more likely to serve in the war zones than were college graduates.[17] It follows that college graduates are more likely to be employed than are high school dropouts.

Again we are reminded of the unequal burden of the war on income and social groups. In response to the charge that blacks and Spanish-surname soldiers experienced disproportionately high casualty rates in the war (e.g.,

Table 7.1
Employment Status of Male Vietnam-Era Veterans Age 25 and Over,[1] by Period of Service, Presence of Service-Connected Disability, and Disability Rating, November 1987 (Not Seasonally Adjusted)

[Numbers in thousands]

Period of service, presence of disability, and disability rating	Civilian noninstitutional population	Civilian labor force					Not in labor force
		Total	Percent of population	Employed	Unemployed		
					Number	Percent of labor force	
Total, Vietnam era							
With service-connected disability	811	633	78.1	594	39	6.2	178
Less than 30-percent disability rating	469	432	92.1	404	27	6.3	38
30- to 50-percent disability rating	170	120	70.6	112	8	6.7	50
60-percent or higher disability rating	129	42	32.6	41	1	(2)	87
Disability rating not reported	43	39	(2)	36	3	(2)	4
Without service-connected disability	6,798	6,409	94.3	6,107	302	4.7	389
Presence of disability not reported	293	256	87.4	250	6	2.2	37
Vietnam theater							
With service-connected disability	529	420	79.4	395	25	5.9	109
Less than 30-percent disability rating	304	276	90.8	257	19	6.8	28
30- to 50-percent disability rating	103	80	77.7	79	2	2.5	21
60-percent or higher disability rating	90	36	40.0	34	1	(2)	55
Disability rating not reported	32	28	(2)	24	3	(2)	4
Without service-connected disability	3,188	2,986	93.7	2,829	156	5.2	202
Presence of disability not reported	118	108	91.5	106	2	1.6	10
Outside Vietnam theater							
With service-connected disability	282	213	75.5	198	14	6.8	69
Less than 30-percent disability rating	165	156	94.5	147	9	5.5	10
30- to 50-percent disability rating	67	40	(2)	34	6	(2)	28
60-percent or higher disability rating	38	7	(2)	7	(2)	(2)	32
Disability rating not reported	11	11	(2)	11	(2)	(2)	2
Without service-connected disability	3,610	3,424	94.8	3,278	146	4.3	186
Presence of disability not reported	175	148	84.6	144	4	2.7	27

[1] Because of the aging of the population, there were no longer any Vietnam-era veterans under 25 years of age.   [2] Data not shown where base is less than 75,000.

Source: Sharon R. Cohany, "Employment and Unemployment among Vietnam-Era Veterans," *Monthly Labor Review* 113 (April 1990): 24.

blacks constituted 9.3 percent of personnel, they suffered 12.6 percent of the deaths), the VA concluded:

> Our sense of the data, however, is that while minority Americans may have suffered a disproportionate share of the exposure to combat and combat fatalities, their suffering was not the product of racial discrimination, but of discrimination against the poor, the uneducated, the young, regardless of their racial or ethnic heritage.[18]

Such candor is rarely found emanating from public agencies. Without dwelling on the issue, it is clear that many undocumented costs are associated with this disclosure, costs that cannot be measured perhaps, but costs nevertheless.

Where are the Vietnam veterans likely to be employed? Nearly two decades after the first reduction of armed forces, the distribution of veterans among industries is similar to that of nonveterans. There is, however, one striking exception: public service employment. Table 7.2 presents these interesting data: 21.5 percent of the Vietnam veterans were employed in the public sector, 9 percent at the federal level, and 12.5 percent at the state and local level. Compare these ratios with the nonveteran of 12.3 percent in total with only 2.1 percent at the federal level. For the disabled, the proportion is much higher: 23.1 percent (30 percent for the seriously disabled) of the Vietnam-era veterans are employed by the federal government. The federal government has clearly been in the forefront in giving preference to and seeking out the disabled veteran.

Vietnam veterans were distributed among occupations in much the same way as nonveterans. Table 7.3 shows the general distribution of veterans by broad occupational groups. Veterans appear more heavily represented in the clerical fields, protective services, and managerial areas and unrepresented in the professions and machine operators.

The problems and challenges forced upon the returning veteran were many and diverse. A few of these problems, bearing mainly on the economic factors, have been suggested here. To continue the discussion would only serve to create additional frustration caused by the inability to complete the accounting for costs that could be attributed to the Vietnam war.[19]

THE PEACE DIVIDEND

Recall that the end of the war was supposed to result in a peace dividend. Funds no longer needed to finance the war could have resulted in a

Table 7.2
Employed Male Vietnam-Era Veterans Age 25 and Over,[1] by Class of Worker and Disability Status, November 1987 (Not Seasonally Adjusted)

[Percent distribution]

Period of service and disability status[2]	Total employed (thousands)	Wage and salary workers				Self-employed and unpaid family workers
		Private	Government			
			Total	Federal	State and local	
Vietnam era	6,951	68.6	21.5	9.0	12.5	9.9
Disabled, total	594	56.1	35.9	23.1	12.8	7.9
Less than 30 percent	404	58.7	34.4	21.0	13.6	6.9
30 percent or more	154	46.8	44.2	31.2	12.3	9.0
Not disabled	6,107	69.9	20.1	7.7	12.4	10.0
Vietnam theater	3,331	66.8	22.4	9.9	12.5	10.7
Disabled, total	395	57.5	33.9	21.3	12.4	8.6
Less than 30 percent	257	61.1	33.5	20.2	13.2	5.4
30 percent or more	113	46.9	40.7	26.5	14.2	12.4
Not disabled	2,829	68.2	21.0	8.4	12.6	10.8
Outside Vietnam theater	3,620	70.3	20.6	8.1	12.5	9.1
Disabled, total	198	53.0	39.9	26.8	13.1	6.6
Less than 30 percent	147	54.4	36.1	22.4	14.3	8.8
30 percent or more	40	(3)	(3)	(3)	(3)	(3)
Not disabled	3,278	71.5	19.3	7.1	12.2	9.2
Nonveterans, 25 years and over	35,313	75.8	12.3	2.1	10.2	11.9

[1] Because of the aging of the population, there were no longer any Vietnam-era veterans under 25 years of age.

[2] Categories may not sum to totals, because information on presence and degree of disability was not reported for some veterans.

[3] Data not shown where base is less than 75,000.

Source: Sharon R. Cohany, "Employment and Unemployment among Vietnam-Era Veterans," *Monthly Labor Review* 113 (April 1990): 26.

reduction in defense spending that could have been made available to the American public for alternative uses. It could have been possible to return the funds to the private sector by reducing taxes; or alternatively, government expenditures could have been increased in other areas, or social programs could have been enhanced. Choices had to be made, of course, since the funds that would be made available would not suffice to satisfy everyone's wish list of things to do.

In March 1967, the president created the Cabinet Coordinating Committee on Economic Planning for the End of Vietnam Hostilities to study the economic consequences of the ending of the war in Southeast Asia.[20] Its report, issued as part of *The Economic Report of the President, 1969*, examined the macroeconomic policies that would be required when the war ended. Depending on just how the war ended, the proper monetary and fiscal policies were suggested that would

Table 7.3
Employed Male Vietnam-Era Veterans and Nonveterans Age 25 and Over,[1] by Occupation, November 1987 (Not Seasonally Adjusted)

[Percent distribution]

Occupation	Vietnam-era veterans			Nonveterans
	Total	Vietnam theater	Outside Vietnam theater	
Total, 25 years and over (in thousands)	6,951	3,331	3,620	35,313
Percent	100.0	100.0	100.0	100.0
Managerial and professional specialty	27.3	25.5	29.0	28.2
Executive, administrative, and managerial	16.8	16.4	17.2	14.3
Professional specialty	10.4	9.0	11.7	13.9
Technical, sales, and administrative support	21.3	21.6	21.0	19.0
Technicians and related support	3.8	3.4	4.3	2.8
Sales occupations	10.4	10.1	10.6	11.1
Administrative support, including clerical	7.1	8.1	6.1	5.1
Service occupations	8.4	8.3	8.5	7.7
Protective service	4.6	4.7	4.6	2.3
Other service occupations	3.8	3.6	3.9	5.5
Precision production, craft, and repair	22.1	21.6	22.7	20.4
Mechanics and repairers	8.3	8.0	8.6	—
Construction trades	7.9	7.5	8.2	—
Other precision production, craft, and repair	5.9	6.1	5.8	—
Operators, fabricators, and laborers	18.7	20.5	17.1	20.1
Machine operators, assemblers, and inspectors	6.9	7.4	6.5	7.9
Transportation and material moving occupations	8.0	9.1	6.9	7.1
Handlers, equipment cleaners, helpers, and laborers	3.9	4.0	3.7	5.1
Farming, forestry, and fishing	2.2	2.6	1.8	4.6

[1] Because of the aging of the population, there were no longer any Vietnam-era veterans under 25 years of age.

NOTE: Dashes indicate data not available.

Source: Sharon R. Cohany, "Employment and Unemployment among Vietnam-Era Veterans," *Monthly Labor Review* 113 (April 1990): 26.

stabilize the economy from any shocks caused by the cessation of hostilities.[21] As interesting as a discussion of these macroeconomic policies might be, they must remain for the more curious since actual events have made them irrelevant.

Concentrating on the peace dividend, the Committee's estimate of the peace dividend with an allowance for growth was about $22 billion for fiscal year 1972. This amount was calculated assuming no new defense programs would be initiated and defense spending would return to baseline expenditures without Vietnam.[22] The committee had many suggestions for alternative uses of the dividend, and even provided a list of programs totalling some $40 billion that could serve as an illustration of the possible uses to which the additional funds could be put. The programs included more expenditures on education, health, environment, urban development, and so on. There appeared to be quite a list of unmet social needs that could absorb the peace dividend and more.

But the peace dividend was not to be. It vanished before any new expenditures or tax reductions could be even debated. Where did it go? The Department of Defense provided the answer—it remained in defense spending. The DOD calculated that reductions in defense spending would have made available some $24 billion but that military pay increases for the remaining personnel and added cost of military retirements used up $16.3 billion, and purchase inflation of 22 percent used up $6.2 billion. The reductions of $24 billion in manpower and purchases were absorbed by increases in defense costs of $22.5 billion leaving only $1.5 billion in net reductions of defense spending.[23]

So much for the peace dividend, and all the pains taken and confusion created in calculating incremental costs that were to be available for peacetime uses at the conclusion of the war. The unmet social needs would remain unmet, more casualties of the war that nobody wanted.

SUMMARY AND CONCLUSIONS

The post-Vietnam society was certainly a different one from the one that existed in the mid-1960s. The structure of the economy changed the operation of the economic system in many ways as inflation forced everyone to adjust plans where possible and learn to adapt to rapidly changing conditions. Inflation and war are eternal partners but the situation in this period is different from past wartime episodes. This was not an all-out war where the entire society was involved and resources for the consumer sector had to be sacrificed. The burden on the private sector was minimal with the main effect being that some individuals had to adjust their portfolios as inflation continued. Others, mainly workers, saw their real incomes fall, but the increase in employment over the period lifted many others who might have suffered unemployment. The redistributions of income are thus difficult to determine, and who won or lost in the inflationary spiral is not all that clear. Creditors lost and debtors gained, at least until new contracts were written or the old ones rewritten.

The situation was complicated by the problem of energy sources, usually taken for granted, becoming uncertain with firms having to adapt their production processes to avoid interruptions. Then with rising energy and food prices and declining real wages, family living standards dropped, and to protect them, secondary workers were necessary. Secondary workers meant mainly wives, and this led to further problems. Family relations had to change, day care for children became a problem, and so on. Again one should not attribute these changes entirely to the war and inflation, but clearly some part of change in participation rates in the labor force can be traced to economic conditions that were the result of a long chain of reactions.

Macroeconomic policy-making in response to these conditions were basically inappropriate. Traditional monetary and fiscal policies simply could not work against stagflation. The price shocks of oil and food could not be controlled by orthodox macroeconomic policies. In fact, they only made matters worse, driving up interest rates or resorting to recessions in order to moderate prices. Of course, faith in macroeconomic policy-making plummeted and with it the liberalism that fostered it. Government became the problem for many and when Ronald Reagan made this a slogan in his campaign of 1980, many could agree with the accusation.

In conclusion, it is apparent that the nation would never be the same following the Vietnam War. Parts of its economic structure were altered, segments of its society were alienated, third parties suffered from manifestations of that alienation, military strategies were gradually changed, and government as a solver of problems was questioned. Macroeconomic policy-making was made suspect, and liberalism was reeling. These conditions set the stage for a different approach to government, and the criticisms made by conservatives found more and more acceptance culminating in the Reagan victory in 1980.

The long chain of events before and after the war changed the economy and society along the way, but the precise accounting for them may never be accomplished. It is never possible to know what would have happened anyway, and the war may have just hastened the changes, but surely some of the postwar changes suggested here can be attributed to the aftermath of war giving us this painful period.

NOTES

1. See Alan S. Blinder, *Economic Policy and the Great Stagflation* (New York: Academic Press, 1979).

2. From March to July, the Federal Reserve required all lenders to maintain a deposit at a Federal Reserve Bank equal to a percentage of credit-card loans and unsecured consumer credit. These reserves were supposed to curb consumer lending and thereby provide some restraint on consumer spending.

3. Abbas Alnasrawi, *OPEC in a Changing World Economy* (Baltimore: Johns Hopkins University Press, 1985), 65–67.

4. Ibid., 97.

5. For more on the housing issue see, Lawrence B. Smith, Kenneth T. Rosen, and George Fallis, "Recent Developments in Economic Models of Housing Markets," in *Journal of Economic Literature*, American Economic Association 26 (March 1988): 29–64, and Dwight R. Lee, "More Costly Housing No Cause for Alarm," *Wall Street Journal*, August 10, 1988, 16. Professor Lee also suggests that in addition to spending more on housing due to the subsidies involved, we built larger houses than would have been the case without the housing distortions.

6. For a useful discussion on the saving rate in the United States see Lawrence Summers and Chris Carroll, "Why is U.S. National Saving So Low?" in *Brookings Papers on Economic Activity* 2 (1987): 607–42.

7. Dwight Lee, "More Costly Housing No Cause for Alarm." He cites a study that found that if the true social rate of return had governed investment, 25 percent less would have been devoted to housing, and other capital stock would have grown by 12 percent with the result that the GNP would have been larger in the years studied.

8. See for instance Ira C. Magaziner and Robert B. Reich, *Minding America's Business* (New York: Vintage Books, 1983); and Barry Bluestone and Bennett Harrison, *The Deindustrialization of America* (New York: Basic Books, 1982).

9. Michael T. Klare, "A Blueprint for Endless Intervention," *Nation*, July 30/August 6, 1988, 77, 95–98.

10. There are many books that discuss the problems of the returning Vietnam War veteran. For a case study approach see, Murray Polner, *No Victory Parades: The Return of the Vietnam Veteran* (New York: Holt, Rinehart and Winston, 1971); and the analysis of Herbert Hendin and Ann Pollinger Haas, *Wounds of War: The Psychological Aftermath of Combat in Vietnam* (New York: Basic Books, 1984); for a clinical approach, John P. Wilson, *Identity, Ideology and Crisis: The Vietnam Veteran in Transition, Part II* (Cleveland, Ohio: Cleveland State University, 1978); for attitudes and perceptions about the war see Ellen Frey-Wouters and Robert S. Laufer, *Legacy of a War* (Armonk, NY: M. E. Sharpe, 1986).

11. Elizabeth Waldman and Kathryn R. Gover, "Employment Situation of Vietnam Era Veterans," *Monthly Labor Review* 94 (September 1971): 3–11.

12. Veterans Administration, *Myths and Realities: A Study of Attitudes Toward Vietnam Era Veterans*, submitted to U.S. House of Representatives, 96th Congress, 2d Session, July 1980, 237, 239.

13. Waldman and Gover, 9.

14. For more on the GI Bill, see *Myths and Realities*, 192–97.

15. Waldman and Gover, 5.

16. Sharon R. Cohany, "Labor Force Status of Vietnam-era Veterans," *Monthly Labor Review* 110 (February 1987): 11–17; and "Employment and Unemployment among Vietnam-era Veterans," *Monthly Labor Review* 113 (April 1990): 22–29.

17. *Myths and Realities*, 10.

18. Ibid., 7.

19. For more detailed analysis of the problems faced by, or are still facing, the Vietnam Veteran, see *Myths and Realities*.

20. The committee was composed of the secretaries of Treasury, Defense, Commerce, and Labor, along with the director of the Budget, and the chairman of the Council of Economic Advisors.

21. The report is an appendix to the *Economic Report of the President, 1969*, 187–211. The monetary and fiscal policies suggested during demobilization can be found in pages 191–98.

22. Ibid., 200–206.

23. U.S. Department of Defense (Comptroller), *The Economics of Defense Spending: A Look at the Realities* (Washington D.C.: U.S. Government Printing Office, July 1972), 150.

8 SUMMARY AND CONCLUSIONS

The September 1988 issue of *Newsweek* carried the headline, "Will We Ever Get over the '60s?" The article referred to much more than the economic consequences—the drug culture, the participation in the war, and all other elements of the radicalism of the period—but adapting that headline to our analysis would find that there is no unambiguous answer to that question. The immediate economic consequences of the war have long since been registered. They were recorded in price statistics, GNP data, unemployment rates, interest rates, and the like. This is not to infer that we recognized all the costs and benefits of the war, only that they became part of the record, whether or not they were perceived as war-induced.

Yet there may still be strands remaining from the period that continue to influence the present. Like a partially destroyed but still intricate cobweb, there may remain portions that cling to the host structure. Unlike the cobweb that is now dormant, however, the remaining strands of earlier economic actions may be strong enough to change the host structure itself. So in this final chapter, it is necessary to pull together some of the immediate economic consequences and distinguish them from the longer run consequences.

LONG-RUN ECONOMIC CONSEQUENCES

Inflation was clearly a short-run consequence of the war. No one doubts that fact. There is some question, however, as to whether or not inflation over a longer-run period can be attributed to the war. The view expressed here is that the original demand side inflation was allowed to permeate the economic system and become cost push inflation. That is, sellers of output or labor began to demand higher rewards as a result of inflation that they did not create. Seeing no remedy for the inflation, and no commitment by government to curtail it, many began to protect themselves from its effects. Inflationary expectations developed and grew unchecked in an atmosphere of confusion and uncertainty.

In response some institutional changes were made over the long term. The banking sector clearly recognized the need for protection from future bouts of inflation. Variable interest rates on mortgages soon made their appearance, certificates of deposit were established, off-shore banking increased, and Eurodollars grew in importance—all in response to previous credit crunches designed to curb inflation. As soon as the government revealed its desire to fight inflation, the banking sector was not far behind in proposing ways to circumvent those policies. The move toward monetarism merely confirmed the suspicions of the banking community that means had to be found to avoid the possible harsher consequences of the fervent application of its principles.

The banking sector responses to inflation were not isolated as others sought to protect themselves as well. Escalator clauses in labor contracts that insured that wages would be adjusted for inflation became more popular, and even Social Security recipients were rewarded in 1975 by Congress when their benefits were tied to the inflation rate. The guideposts of the Kennedy administration were an early victim of inflation, but another scheme was instituted by the Carter administration. There was continued interest in new approaches to control prices and wages, including indexing all rewards by the rate of inflation, tax-based incomes policies, and so on. None of these schemes were ever enacted, but they do show the extent of the concern for inflation, and the readiness of many to combat it with institutional changes. While there was much interest in incomes policies, the actual experience with controls, either direct or voluntary, has made any attempt to reimpose any scheme highly unlikely.

In the fight against inflation, so feared by so many, one of the most powerful weapons to use against it was surrendered in past battles that used inept programs. The guideposts, the wage and price controls of the Nixon administration, and the Carter experimentation with voluntary controls, all were regarded as failures, and likely to do more harm than good. Despite their considerable flaws, these incomes policies were judged on how they worked in practice and not how they would have worked had they been designed better and administered with care and enthusiasm. Past incomes policies were ill-conceived, ill-designed, and ill-administered, and in the case of the Nixon controls system, designed to achieve other noneconomic purposes. That they failed is not a surprise but with their failure we surrendered incomes policies in general as a means to control inflation. Presumably they had been tried and found wanting.

The nation's responses to the energy crisis have been outlined earlier. The inflationary period of the 1960s in the United States precipitated the response of OPEC that caused the energy problems of the 1970s. The immediate types of reactions can easily be recounted—more insulation, more efficient appliances, more fuel efficient, smaller autos, and so on but the longer-run reactions of firms to changes in their operations are not as clear and remain to be examined. With the disappearance of the oil problem in the 1980s went the immediate concern for energy as a national problem. National attention was directed at the safety and operation of nuclear energy plants, and shifted away from longer-run issues. Problems with the ozone layers, greenhouse effects, and acid rain may bring long-run concerns back to the forefront of national concerns, but simply reacting to crises is not conducive to rational solutions.

In the area of macroeconomic policy, the main legacy of the inflation of the 1960s and 70s is the rejection of government policies because they may either cause or exacerbate inflation. This fear is due first to the erroneous belief that government spending always causes deficits and second that budget deficits cause inflation. Neither of these beliefs are necessarily true, but they became part of the conventional wisdom until the 1980s. A more Machiavellian view would suggest that these beliefs were deliberately fostered by conservatives to support the argument for less government spending. When the link between deficits and inflation was severed in the 1980s, fear of increasing the budget deficit took its place as the rationale for not creating new programs or adequately funding the old ones.

The practical effect, however, regardless of the origin of the beliefs about government spending and inflation is that many programs were forestalled for fear of causing or reigniting inflation. Many social programs were not initiated because of inflation, and many were not pursued once they were begun. Again the fear of inflation is a convenient excuse for not doing something about social concerns. Even as these concerns, inadequate and insufficient housing, health care, drug abuse, and so on, became public and caused a public outcry, budgetary effects took precedence over compassion.

In addition, the use of fiscal policy, long identified with liberalism, was downgraded. Government attempts to employ its powers to manage the economy by altering its budget were deemed too risky. Inflation might result. Consequently in a recession, when the proper fiscal policy might be to increase public spending or reduce taxation, there was a reluctance even then to use the available methods. Instead monetary policy with its selective effectiveness was used. It is not wise to abandon the use of one element of macroeconomic policy and rely solely on the other. Not only will the method employed be less effective having to do the job alone, but many will recognize the reliance on the one policy and make adjustments to free themselves from its effects. The result is much less effective macroeconomic policy in general, and selective impacts on segments of the economy in particular. Those who can avail themselves of protection will do so, and those who cannot will bear the brunt of the policy.

An illustration of the latter group would be those who expected the society to address their needs, and who were bitterly disappointed when it did not. The war on poverty presumably could no longer be afforded in an inflationary period when more urgent expenditures on the other war were required. Many disadvantaged saw their hopes dashed as the promises made to them went unfulfilled. The blacks too saw their expectations for advancement and for greater participation in the economy sacrificed as well. The continued social problems associated with these groups attests to the longer-run consequences of failure to confront the problems earlier—inflation or no. The Great Society became the Indifferent Society, more concerned with price stability than human advancement and dignity.

Whether or not the funds used in the war effort would have been redirected to social programs is problematical; there is no assurance that there was a direct shift of funds away from social concerns to defense needs. In other words, had there been no war, would we have spent the funds used in Southeast Asia on domestic programs that would have aided the disadvantaged and extended the New Deal as Johnson wished? Obviously, much would depend on the willingness of Congress to allocate more funds to the Great Society. Many people had a list of unmet social needs where the funds could be absorbed easily, and these were known at the time of the military buildup.[1]

There is no way to replay history, and thus no answer to the question of how Congress would have reacted to requests for additional funds for the war on poverty. All that can be inferred is that with the prevailing attitude at the time toward redressing some of society's ills, it is likely that Congress would have gone along with additional funding requests. It is not at all clear that it would have been willing to spend over $140 billion on such efforts. Sooner or later, Mr. Johnson's magic with Congress would have disappeared, and the early triumphs would not have been repeated. The conclusion is a weak one, then, since all that can be suggested is that some of the funds spent on the war might have been redirected toward social programs, but not to the extent of the actual amounts spent in Southeast Asia. Our generosity in peace is never matched by our fervor in war.

The greater tragedy, however, may not be in what was left undone, but in the belief that we had done all we could do and failed. We tried to fight poverty and lost, so why keep trying. From this view it is easy to blame the victim and absolve society or the economic system. Inadequate funding would not be seen as the reason for failure, nor would comparisons between the amounts spent on the war and on domestic problems be deemed relevant. In the end we lost both wars, but would admit to neither. While the Vietnam War had its own aftermath, the war on poverty could take comfort in the Biblical admonition—the poor will always be with us.

BENEFITS VERSUS COSTS

Inflation costs are easy to measure compared with the costs of disrupted lives. The costs during the war and after, both to those who participated directly and to those who remained behind, are too often ignored. Yet so many lives were touched, that some acknowledgment of the burden is imperative.

For those who remained behind, the task is virtually impossible. We simply cannot know what plans were postponed, what plans were cancelled, or what plans were reconsidered. Some jobs were taken, for example, that were not really wanted and some jobs were passed up because they conflicted with travel plans; some women moved to be near members of the armed forces, and others remained at home but were awaiting news of future homes, and were reluctant to enter into long-run commitments. How many women postponed their education and careers, and how many undertook careers while waiting for their loved ones to return, careers they may not have pursued, except that time was available? When families were reunited, how many lives of women and children were destroyed by veterans who could not adjust to civilian life? Surely some of these decisions must have involved economic costs but the question is how to identify them, and even more difficult, how to evaluate and measure them. There is no calculus for these disruptions, and no way to quantify them, but they were real nevertheless. Yet it is interesting to note that *women's views on the war and its aftermath are seldom solicited*. It is almost as if we dare not expose the degree of indirect and intangible costs of the war to greater scrutiny.

For those who served more directly in the armed forces, similar costs are involved. Some postponed their education or careers and were prevented from getting started in the fulfillment of their long-run plans. Those who were drafted received lower incomes and paid a special tax in the form of delayed entrance into the workforce and reduced earnings in the long run. When they returned, they paid again with a host of adjustment problems ranging from drug addiction and crime to suicide and alcoholism. All of these problems are potential destroyers of life, and all have an economic cost attached to them, whether measurable or not.

Not all members of the armed forces saw combat, of course, and adjustment problems may not apply to them. Still some of them postponed educational opportunities and career choices, and economic costs are applicable. Others, however, may have benefited from their experience in the armed forces if they received training they otherwise would not have had. Training and skills learned in the armed forces could carry over into civilian life and enable the person to earn a higher reward or be eligible for a better job. In these cases, the benefits may outweigh the costs.

Still others would register neither extensive costs or benefits. Such individuals lived through their experience without severe disruption or beneficial opportunities. Some even found the military suitable for a career after their exposure to it.

In sum, the longer-run economic costs of participation in the war can never be known with precision. For what it is worth, the only available evidence suggests that the costs to individuals exceed the benefits.[2] There are no data on the economic costs imposed on those less directly involved; the data are neither collected nor even deemed relevant. It is not even clear whether these costs will disappear with the passage of time. Children were affected as well by problems they did not create, and they could easily perpetuate them for a long time afterwards. As the war experience recedes in our memories, the problems may seem unconnected to the original source and even more difficult to trace and understand. A child beaten by a returning veteran may beat his children, etc.

Wars, hot or cold, generally stimulate an economic system. The Vietnam War was no exception. As the war progressed, the unemployment rate fell, from 4.5 percent in 1965 to a low of 3.3 percent in early 1969. Falling rates of unemployment are usually considered desirable, especially when they record the employment of the long-term unemployed, the disadvantaged, and minorities. Overheating in the economy is good news for these groups—the last in, first out, members of the labor force.

Hence the wartime economy must be credited with bringing benefits to one important segment of the labor force. The war succeeded in creating employment opportunities that were unavailable in the absence of stimulation. The question for us is whether or not the post–tax-cut economy of 1964 would have accomplished the same thing. The prewar economy was showing signs of renewed strength, and employment gains appeared likely to accompany the economic growth. No answer for this question exists, and one may not ever be possible.

Still, even if some short-run benefits are assumed, the longer-run benefits seem to disappear. Once the economy had adjusted and returned to more stable conditions, unemployment returned to previous levels as well. The early 1970s saw the rate returned to the 5 percent range, and even higher rates were recorded as the decade progressed. There do not appear to be any lasting gains for the labor force as a whole, although individuals or groups may have received longer-term gains.

In addition to these factors, there is the question of the debt incurred in order to finance the war. As recounted earlier, the war was not financed by taxation. What little taxes were collected were not sufficient to cover the cost of the war. The Revenue and Expenditure Control Act of 1968, the only real tax measure designed in response to the war, actually produced only $21 billion dollars in additional revenue.[3] Over the period 1965–72, there were deficits totaling $61.5 billion, and an addition to the public debt of $85.9 billion. Clearly some of the increase in the debt must be attributed to the financing of the Vietnam War, although the exact relation cannot be determined. Again the exact measurement is not the issue; the burden of this debt is the problem.

Since most of this debt was held internally, the burden of the debt is generally held to be minimal. When it is repaid, the taxpayers turn over funds to the bondholders, and while there may be some redistributional effects, the amounts transferred remain in the country. However the real question is not the usual burden argument, but what did we get for the increase in the public debt? If the debt were incurred to stimulate the economy in a period of recession, the benefits of a thriving economy can be readily apparent, easily understood, and perhaps even socially acceptable. Or some other motivation could have prompted the incurring of debt to permit spending on other programs deemed desirable. The economy did not need stimulation at the time of the military buildup, however, and large deficits were not necessary to revive the economy. So what did we get for the portion of the debt identified with the war in Southeast Asia? This war was not socially acceptable, such that people were willing to borrow to finance it and use resources, men and materiel etc., for the stated objectives of the conflict. The fact is that even proponents of the involvement in Southeast Asia would admit that it involved a great deal of waste of resources. These resources could have been employed in domestic invest- ment, so needed for growth, or employed in research, development, or production of other goods. In short, future generations could well end up with fewer goods and services, a smaller capital stock, and higher taxes to pay for a war that produced few benefits.

True the wartime economy boomed, and many benefited at the time. Some of these people, or their descendants who benefited indirectly, may also be involved in paying back the debt. For others, however, this will not be the case, and they may well wonder if the funds used for the war could not have been put to better use. This is not to deny that similar concerns might be expressed if the funds used in the war were spent on domestic social programs instead. These expenditures, however, probably would have received more widespread approval and social acceptability. Expen- ditures made in Southeast Asia were not socially acceptable but indeed, were very divisive and contentious. The benefits from social expenditures might also have proved beneficial to future generations, but there is no way of knowing this in the absence of knowledge of how the funds would have been spent.

It is likely that the military industrial complex benefited from the war. The military industrial complex should be understood to include organized labor and major universities in the United States.[4] Many defense contracts were awarded in which various elements of the complex benefited in varying degrees. Identifying the exact amounts attributed to just the war would be difficult, but fortunately that is not the purpose of this section. It is sufficient to identify the groups who could have benefited from the existence of war. That defense contractors would be one such group is not likely to surprise anyone, but large parts of organized labor were behind the war, and universities and individual professors were also beneficiaries of government contracts for research and development for the military as well as social science applications designed to acquaint officials with the culture, social and economic systems, and history of our opponents. Student demonstrations at these institutions failed to stop the research, but they did succeed in calling attention to one aspect of wartime activity usually ignored—the subversion of the universities and the diversion of research toward military applications and away from pure or socially useful applications.

According to radical reasoning, we should look for rationales other than the stated ones to explain wars. Stopping the spread of communism, or preventing the dominoes from falling, were the official explanations for U.S. involvement in Southeast Asia. Containing China was another reason given for the war, but this seemed less credible then and even less now.[5]

However, beneath the surface explanation should be a discernible rationale that relates to imperialism, and the exploitation of resources or markets by the dominant power. Again one looks in vain for the imperialism motivation since there were no resources to exploit or markets to control. Whatever perceived benefits these may have conferred on the United States, they are not observable in either the short or long run. Stopping the spread of communism, however questionable or irrational, appears to be the main impetus for the conflict. Of course, this is nothing more than an extension of the Truman Doctrine of containment.

Another rationale is much more discernible if one discards the old excuses for war. It was, to quote Sartre, a "war of example"; "Americans want to show others that guerilla war does not pay: they want to show all the oppressed and exploited nations that might be tempted to shake off the American yoke. . . . In short, they want to show Latin America first of all, and more generally, all of the Third World."[6]

But the costs of the war became too great. Once it became clear that an easy victory and a quick end of the war was unattainable, frustration was inevitable. The public grew impatient, the politicians grew more belligerent, and the youth grew more radical. After more troops, more bombing, and more defoliation were ineffective, disillusionment set in, and the scramble was on to get out, presumably with honor. No one had bargained for a long, costly, and protracted war where justification would be questioned.

So, when the war was lost, there was the utter sense of futility—for nothing was achieved. No land was annexed, no markets were opened for exploitation, and no resources were made more readily available. There were no falling dominoes, no Asian blocks, no China containment (Nixon would soon be opening up relations), and much worse, no demonstration effect on Latin America. Nothing was gained, but a great deal was lost. National pride was wounded, and the society was sharply divided. The result was the evolution of the Vietnam syndrome—the determination to avoid such entanglements in the future.

The Vietnam syndrome, the reluctance to repeat the experience, did have longer-run implications. It lasted until the Reagan administration, as we have seen, when with concerted effort, it was broken by adventures in Central America, the Middle East, Grenada, and Libya. Yet is was not sufficient to break the syndrome, and more observable evidence was required to restore respect for U.S. military might and the military establishment. Apparently the malaise following Vietnam prevented us from keeping our defenses as strong as needed. We had fallen behind, according to Reagan, because we were apologetic over the conflict in Vietnam and foundering in our resolve to be the strongest nation on the globe. We were not asserting ourselves in world affairs, partly because we lacked the will (the syndrome), and partly because we lacked the clout.

To remedy these shortcomings, the Reagan administration proceeded to restore our defenses. It embarked on a long-term plan that would have committed the United States to spend $1.5 trillion in just five years on national defense. The United States would outspend the Soviet Union, the evil empire, and show our willingness to wreck their economy if they chose to match our efforts. It did not even matter whether or not the weapons worked or not; it was the expenditure *on* defense that mattered, not the expenditure *for* defense. The national defense expenditures thus restored the prestige and pride in the military establishment. Given more than enough funds (the Pentagon had to scramble around for projects to spend the funds on) confidence and self-esteem returned to the Pentagon. Distrust in the military and military solutions began to wane. Again the military-industrial complex became the beneficiaries of the breakdown of the Vietnam syndrome; the complex thus gained during the war and by the delayed reactions to it, many years later.

Still it was necessary to use the military power if any credence was to be given to the resurrection of our military presence. Hence the second stage in the treatment for the Vietnam syndrome was the aggressive exercise of military might, and the active role of the United States in international affairs. The results of these actions are not all in, but it is clear that the American public was not always willing to follow the lead of this more aggressive stance. To continue this discussion, however, would take us beyond the purpose of this book. Only the economic consequences of these acts is of concern to us; the resulting budget deficit, caused largely by defense spending, will continue to affect the domestic economy for years to come.

It would be naive to suggest that the war was ended because it was inflicting such a heavy cost on the Vietnamese without inducing surrender.

Still a short discussion of these costs is necessary to suggest the nature of the war from the other side. The destruction of Vietnam was unparalleled,

> but any reasonable estimate must conclude that never before in the history of mankind has such a magnitude of destruction been wrought upon any people, at any time, in any single place. Herbicides, free fire zones, antipersonnel and fragmentation bombs, napalm, urbanization, food denial programs, all together form an unprecedented strategy of counterinsurgency which relies increasingly upon air technology rather than ground combat warfare. The current American destruction of Southeast Asia represents a new and unprecedented strategy, aimed not at the destruction of an enemy, his territory, a food crop or a culture but of an entire ecosystem. This is Ecocide. [Ecocide is the premeditated assault of a nation and its resources against the individuals, culture, and biological fabric of another country and its environs.][7]

These are strong words, but they are still inadequate to express the utter devastation of the country. The whole society was affected as so much of the economic activity was directed to serving the needs of the U.S. military. Women became prostitutes, young boys became houseboys, local politicians became corrupted, some became drug dealers while others became merchants of U.S. made goods on the streets. Civilian casualties were heavy; an estimated 1,050,000 casualties were reported with 325,000 deaths. Thirty percent of the deaths were children under 13 years of age.[8] In addition, some 4–5 million became refugees moving to urban centers at first, and then later trying to flee the country. Still casualty data and dislocation estimates cannot tell the human costs of the war. To tell this story, creative artists of all kinds are needed to remind us of individual tragedies amid the collective statistics.

The economy of South Vietnam suffered as a result of these dislocations as well. Land destruction transformed agriculture, and herbicides threatened not only the current crops but perhaps crops for years after the war. Rice that had been previously exported now had to be imported. Inflation soared as prices increased seven fold from 1965 to 1971; the money supply grew by 150 percent from 1966 to 1970 requiring devaluation to stabilize monetary conditions; and the GNP grew by only 12 percent in the period 1966–69. Clearly the economy was in shambles during the war, and likely to be for years after.[9] Similar problems were felt in Laos and Cambodia as the war expanded into these nations as well. In short the whole social and economic structure of Southeast Asia was transformed by this war.

It is in the nature of economics that conclusions are seldom absolute. So it is with this study. The true economic consequences of the Vietnam War may never be identified. An event such as the Vietnam War disturbs an economic and social system in such a traumatic way that all of the reactions and ramifications that flow from it may never be traceable; and even if the immediate ones can somehow be cataloged, the repercussions may extend far into the future long after the initial cause has ceased. It is a situation appropriate to the pebble in the water metaphor. Still the admission that any study of the economic consequences of the Vietnam War may never be complete should not deter the attempts to approach the task, even if partial answers frustrate the mind.

The main thrust of this study has been to identify some of the immediate consequences of the war and to show how those consequences led to adjustments in the economic system that were severe enough to warrant the claim that the economic structure was transformed. The postwar economy would never be the same as the prewar economy, and furthermore, there would be no tendency to return to the earlier economic structure. There would be no internal mechanisms to steer the economy back to its original path of development.

For example, inflation was ignited in the early stages of the war, and economic policies at first were not initiated, and second, when they were, caused havoc. As a result, economic agents who were severely affected in either or both stages took actions to protect themselves from similar occurrences. These reactions erected new institutions that moved the economy away from the typical reactions of the past. As more and more agents became affected, more and more ways were discovered to avoid or minimize government policies or the reactions of other economic agents who were trying to protect themselves. These institutions were subject to much experimentation as they evolved, but their main purpose was still to insulate themselves from the actions of others.

These maneuvers are not specific to any one period of time, of course, as they have occurred in the past as well. Wars, however, accelerate these innovations, elevate their sophistication, and condense the time required for major revisions to occur. The result over a longer time period is the speeding up of change, sometimes without the participants' knowledge of what is happening. Eventually the initial confusion gives way to acceptance, and the change becomes part of the normal system. It may no longer even be possible to identify why, how, or where the change originated.

The long-term consequences of earlier actions or inactions may now be evident without revealing their sources. The banking sector, for example, reacted to the inflationary period and the credit crunches to establish a host of new monetary instruments, new institutions to deal with the changing problems, new external relations, new international arrangements, and so on. Once changes disturb the basic foundation of how things are done, there is no end to the acceptance of new arrangements. Thus over even a longer period, additional structural changes can be made that go beyond the need for self-protection that precipitated the changes in the first place. There are cumulative, snowballing effects to the acceptance of a modification of past practices or innovation.

It is suggested here that many deviations from the past were brought about rather quickly by the stresses and strains of the Vietnam War, its conduct and its financing. Societal changes have been and will continue to be described by others. Some of the economic consequences, both short and long-term, have been suggested in this study.

NOTES

1. For instance see the statement of Wassily Leontief in Congress of the United States, Joint Economic Committee, Hearings, *Economic Effects of Vietnam Spending*, 90th Congress, 1st session, April 1967, 242–46. See also some later analyses in *The Economic Consequences of Reduced Military Spending* edited by Bernard Udis (Lexington, Mass.: D.C. Heath, 1973).

2. Phillip Cutright, "Achievement, Military Service, and Earnings," unpublished manuscript, May 20, 1969 (Social Security Administration) cited by Larry A. Sjaastad in his, "The Conscription Tax: An Empirical Analysis," in the President's Commission on an *All Volunteer Armed Force*, November 1970.

3. As estimated by the Tax Foundation in its *Tax Features*, 32, no. 1 (January 1988): 2.

4. Sidney Lens, *The Military-Industrial Complex* (Philadelphia: Pilgrim Press, 1970).

5. For an articulate explanation of the war's rationale see, Norman Podhoretz, *Why We Were in Vietnam* (New York: Simon and Schuster, 1982).

6. Jean-Paul Sartre, "On Genocide," in *Ecocide in Indochina: The Ecology of War*, edited by Barry Weisberg (San Francisco: Canfield Press, 1970), 39.

7. Orville Schell and Barry Weisberg, "Ecocide in Indochina," in *Ecocide in Indochina* edited by Barry Weisberg (San Francisco: Canfield Press, 1970), 17–18.

8. U.S. Congress, U.S. Senate, Committee on Foreign Relations, *Impact of the Vietnam War*, 92nd Congress, 1st session, June 30, 1971, 15.

9. Ibid., 35.

SELECT BIBLIOGRAPHY

Agency for International Development. *U.S. Foreign Assistance and Assistance from International Organizations, July 1, 1945–June 30, 1961.*

Bowles, Samuel, David M. Gordon, and Thomas E. Weisskopf. *Beyond the Waste Land.* New York: Anchor/Doubleday, 1983.

Brown, Sam, and Len Ackland, eds. *Why Are We Still in Vietnam?* New York: Random House, 1970.

Chomsky, Noam. *American Power and the New Mandarins.* New York: Pantheon Books, 1967.

Clark, John M. *The Costs of the World War to the American People.* New Haven: Yale University Press, 1931.

Clayton, James L. *The Economic Impact of the Cold War.* New York: Harcourt, Brace & World, 1970.

Cohany, Sharon R. "Labor Force Status of Vietnam-era Veterans." *Monthly Labor Review* 110 (February 1987): 11–17.

————. "Employment and Unemployment among Vietnam-era Veterans." *Monthly Labor Review* 113 (April 1990): 22–29.

Committee for Economic Development. *The National Economy and the Vietnam War.* New York: April 1968.

Committee of Concerned Asian Scholars. *The Indochina Story.* New York: Bantam Books, 1970.

Cornell University Air War Study Group. *The Air War in Indochina*, rev. ed. Boston: Beacon Press, 1972.

Council of Economic Advisors. *Economic Report of the President.* Washington, D.C.: U.S. Government Printing Office, various years.

Denison, Edward F. "Explanations of Declining Productivity Growth." *Survey of Current Business* 59, no. 8 (August 1979): 1–24.

Eckstein, Otto. *Core Inflation.* Englewood Cliffs, N.J.: Prentice-Hall, 1981.

Eisner Robert. "The War and the Economy." In *Why Are We Still In Vietnam?* edited by Sam Brown and Len Ackland. New York: Random House, 1970.

Foner, Philip S. *American Labor and the Indochina War: The Growth of Union Opposition*. New York: International Publishers, 1971.

Frey-Wouters, Ellen, and Robert S. Laufer. *Legacy of a War*. Armonk, N.Y.: M. E. Sharpe, 1986.

Friedman, M., and W. Heller. *Monetary vs. Fiscal Policy*. New York: Norton, 1969.

Garrison, Charles B., and Anne Mayhew. "The Alleged Vietnam War Origins of the Current Inflation: A Comment." *Journal of Economic Issues* 17 (March 1983): 175–86.

Goldwater, Barry M. *With No Apologies*. New York: Morrow, 1979.

Goodwin, Richard N. *Remembering America*. Boston: Little, Brown, 1988.

Grant, J. S., A. G. Moss, and J. Unger. *Cambodia: The Widening War in Indochina: A Primer*. New York: Washington Square Press, 1971.

Halberstam, David. *The Best and the Brightest*. New York: Random House, 1972.

Hartke, Vance. *The American Crisis in Vietnam*. New York: Bobbs-Merrill, 1968.

Heller, Walter. *New Dimensions of Political Economy*. New York: W. W. Norton, 1967.

Karnow, Stanley. *Vietnam: A History*. New York: Viking Press, 1983.

Kearns, Doris. *Lyndon Johnson and the American Dream*. New York: Harper & Row, 1976.

Kerner, Otto. *Report of the National Advisory Commission Civil Disorders*. Washington, D.C.: U.S. Government Printing Office, March 1981.

Klein, Lawrence R. "Econometric Analysis of the Tax Cut of 1964." In *The Brookings Model: Some Further Results*, edited by J. S. Duesenberry, et al., 459–72. Chicago: Rand McNally, 1969.

Koistinen, Paul A. C. *The Military Industrial Complex*. New York: Praeger, 1980.

Kolko, Gabriel. *Anatomy of a War*. New York: Pantheon Books, 1985.

Larsen, Stanley R., and James L. Collins, Jr. *Allied Participation in Vietnam*. Washington, D.C.: Department of the Army, 1975.

Lens, Sidney. *Permanent War*. New York: Schocken Books, 1987.

Levitan, Sar A. *The Great Society's Poor Law: A New Approach to Poverty*. Baltimore: Johns Hopkins Press, 1969.

Magdoff, Harry. "Productivity Slowdown: A False Alarm." *Monthly Review* 31 (June 1979): 1–12.

Melman, Seymour. *Pentagon Capitalism: The Political Economy of War*. New York: McGraw-Hill, 1970.

———, ed. *The War Economy of the United States*. New York: St Martin's Press, 1971.

———. *The Permanent War Economy*. New York: Simon and Schuster, 1974.

Okun, Arthur. *The Political Economy of Prosperity*. New York: W. W. Norton, 1970.

———. "Measuring the Impact of the 1964 Tax Cut" in *Readings in Money, National Income, and Stabilization Policy*, edited by Warren Smith and Ronald L. Teigen, 345–58. Homewood, Ill: Richard D. Irwin, 1970.

———. "The Personal Tax Surcharge and Consumer Demand, 1968–70." *Brookings Papers*, 167–212. Washington, D.C.: The Brookings Institution, 1971.

———. "Did the 1968 Surcharge Really Work?: Comment." *American Economic Review* 67 (March 1977): 166–69.

Plotnick, Robert D., and Felicity Skidmore. *Progress Against Poverty: A Review of the 1964–1974 Decade*. New York: Academic Press, 1975.

Podhoretz, Norman. *Why We Were in Vietnam*. New York: Simon and Schuster, 1982.

President's Commission on an All-Volunteer Armed Force. Washington, D.C.: U.S. Government Printing Office, February 1970.

Russett, Bruce M. *What Price Vigilance?* New Haven: Yale University Press, 1970.

Sheahan, John. *The Wage-Price Guideposts.* Washington, D. C.: The Brookings Institution, 1967.

Sheehan, Neil. *A Bright Shining Lie.* New York: Random House, 1988.

Silk, Leonard. *Nixonomics.* New York: Praeger, 1972.

Solow, Robert M. "The Intelligent Citizen's Guide to Inflation." *The Public Interest* 38 (Winter 1975): 30–66.

Springer, William L. "Did the 1968 Surcharge Really Work?" *American Economic Review* 65 (September 1975): 644–59.

———. "Did the 1968 Surcharge Really Work?: Reply." *American Economic Review* 67 (March 1977): 170–72.

Stevens, Robert Warren. *Vain Hopes, Grim Realities.* New York: New Viewpoints, 1976.

Stone, I. F. *Polemics and Prophecies, 1967–1970.* New York: Random House, 1970.

Taylor, Clyde, ed. *Vietnam and Black America.* New York: Anchor Press/Doubleday, 1973.

Taylor, Leonard B. *Financial Management of the Vietnam Conflict, 1962–1972.* Washington, D.C.: Department of the Army, 1974.

Udis, Bernard, ed. *The Economic Consequences of Reduced Military Spending.* Lexington, Mass.: D.C. Heath, 1973.

U.S. Congress, House of Representatives, Committee on the Budget. *Economic Stabilization Policies: The Historical Record, 1962–76,* Washington, D.C.: U.S. Government Printing Office, November 1978.

U.S. Congress, Joint Economic Committee. *The Economic Effects of Vietnam Spending,* 90th Congress, 1st session, Vol. I, April and July 1967.

———. *The Military Budget and National Economic Priorities,* Hearings, 91st Congress, June 1969.

U.S. Congress, Senate Committee on Foreign Relations, Subcommittee on United States Security Agreements and Commitments Abroad, 91st Congress. *Hearings,* November 1969 and February 1970.

U.S. Department of Defense (Comptroller). *Semiannual Report of the Secretary of Defense, January 1 to June 20, 1954.* Washington, D.C.: U.S. Government Printing Office, 1955.

———. *The Economics of Defense Spending: A Look at the Realities.* Washington D.C.: U.S. Government Printing Office, 1972.

———. *Foreign Military Sales and Military Assistance Facts.* December 1976.

Waldman, Elizbeth, and Kathryn R. Gover. "Employment Situation of Vietnam Era Veterans," *Monthly Labor Review* 94 (September 1971): 3–11.

Walker, John F., and Harold G. Vatter. "The Princess and the Pea; or the Alleged Vietnam War Origins of the Current Inflation," *Journal of Economic Issues* 16 (June 1982): 597–608.

———. "Demonstrating the Undemonstrable," *Journal of Economic Issues* 22 (March 1983): 186–96.

Weidenbaum, Murray L. *Economic Impact of the Vietnam War.* Center for Strategic Studies, Special Report Series No. 5. Georgetown University, Washington, D.C.: Renaissance Editions, June 1967.

———. "Defense Expenditures and the Domestic Economy," in *Defense Management,* edited by Stephen Enke, 317–36. Englewood Cliffs, N.J.: Prentice-Hall, 1967.

Weisberg, Barry, ed. *Ecocide in Indochina: The Ecology of War.* San Francisco: Canfield Press, 1970.

INDEX

About the Author

ANTHONY S. CAMPAGNA is Professor of Economics at the University of Vermont, where he specializes in macroeconomic theory and policy. He is the author of three previous books, including *U.S. National Economic Policy, 1917–1985* (Praeger, 1987).